FROM WORSHIP TO WARFARE

"A thousand may fall at your side, and ten thousand at your right hand,
but it shall not come near you."
Psalm 91:7

Books by Renee Vetter

The Warrior's Legacy, Stories of Deliverance

Intercessory Prayer Handbook

God Got To Me First

Mission Safety Kit

Forever And Ever Amen

Purpose In Your Heart ~ A Youth Bible Study

Purpose In Your Heart ~ A Youth Bible Study Leader's Discussion Guide + Student Workbook

Liberty Ladies ~ A Novel

Books may be purchased at www.HandofGodMinistry.com

FROM WORSHIP TO WARFARE

"A thousand may fall at your side, and ten thousand at your right hand, but it shall not come near you."
Psalm 91:7

By Renee Vetter

Hand of God Ministries
2015

From Worship to Warfare
Copyright © 2020 by Renee Vetter

All rights reserved

ISBN 978-1-67818-621-0

Hand of God Ministries
www.handofgodministry.com
P.O. Box 1685
Boyd, Texas 76023

No part of this publication may be reproduced, stored in a retrieval system, or transmitted in any form or by any means—electronic, mechanical, photocopying, recording, or otherwise--without the prior written consent of the author and/or Hand of God Ministries.

All Scripture quotations, unless otherwise indicated, are taken from the New King James Version®. Thomas Nelson Publishers. Copyright © 1982. Used by permission. All rights reserved.

Scripture quotations marked AMPC are taken from the Amplified® Bible, Classic Edition, Copyright © 1954, 1958, 1962, 1965, 1987 by The Lockman Foundation Used by permission. All rights reserved.

Scripture quotations marked NIV are taken from THE HOLY BIBLE, NEW INTERNATIONAL VERSION®, NIV® Copyright © 1973, 1978, 1984 Biblica. Zondervan Publishing Used by permission. All rights reserved.

Scripture quotations marked NLT are taken from the Holy Bible, New Living Translation, Copyright © 1996, 2004, 2007 by the Tyndale House Foundation. Used by permission of Tyndale House Publishers. All rights reserved.

Scripture quotations marked TLB are taken from the The Living Bible. Copyright © 1971 by the Tyndale House Publishers. Used by permission. All rights reserved.

TABLE OF CONTENTS

FORWARD

Chapter 1
PURPOSE IN YOUR HEART

Chapter 2
THE LORD WILL NOT SHARE HIS THRONE WITH ANOTHER

Chapter 3
WORSHIP WILL TAKE YOU WHERE KNOWLEDGE CANNOT KEEP YOU

Chapter 4
GOD REVEALS HIS SECRETS

Chapter 5
SUDDENLY THERE WAS A GREAT EARTHQUAKE

Chapter 6
"MY PEOPLE ARE DESTROYED FOR LACK OF KNOWLEDGE."

Chapter 7
"I BELIEVED THEREFORE I SPOKE."

FOREWORD

Psalm 26:8 *"Lord, I have loved the habitation of Your house and the place where Your glory dwells."*

To me, worship is being in the presence of the Lord, sensing His majesty, feeling His love, and experiencing His mercy. Psalm 26:8 is one of my favorite verses because when I speak those words it is almost as if the throne room of God envelops me and I expect to see His glory at any moment. The Lord has placed such a spirit of expectation within me that I expect to see His glory all around me.

Your church, whatever denomination it happens to be, is the house of the Lord, but we also are called the *"temple of the Holy Spirit."* So the glory dwells within us, as well as in the church. No matter where I am when I arise in the morning, I put on some praise music, take my Bible and get alone and quiet before God. That is where the potential is to walk into His glory. He is so vast yet so personal, so magnificent yet so attainable. The Creator of the heavens and earth will sing to you through anointed praise music and the air becomes thick with the presence of the living God.

Have you learned to worship losing all sense of time and just desiring to see His face and be pleasing in His sight? I desire to see my Father smile at me with love and recognition, eager to see me and spend time with me. There is nothing like worshiping God in the *"beauty of His holiness."*

One day I will walk into His presence and never come back out. Until that day comes, I am determined to adore Him and praise Him and let Him take me from glory to glory while He changes me into the image of His son. Hallelujah!

Worship is adoration of God and the glorifying of King Jesus who sits at the right hand of God. I pray that this book will teach

§
Worshiping God lets us feel His power all around us.

§
Warfare is God using His power through us by His Holy Spirit

you and lead you into worship. The ability to worship God does not just happen. It takes work, sacrifice, adaptability, and a tender heart towards the things of God. It takes a desire to be less of you and more of Him.

David was called a man after God's own heart. He was a worshiper and as David grew, he became a warrior. Worshiping God lets us feel His power all around us. Warfare is God using His power through us by His Holy Spirit. When God is ready for us to live in His throne room, He'll bring us home, but until then we have a mission to fulfill on the earth.

A worshiper without warring will seldom see victory; and a warrior who does not worship will lose sight of Who is on the throne. One without the other is a lopsided gospel. The world does not see Christians as victorious because their lives are filled with the same problems and weaknesses as those who are non-Christian. The world sees our leaders falling into adultery, addictions of all kinds, or in many instances divorce. They are witnessing in some cases a meltdown of the church because of the acceptance of sin and the lifestyle that it brings. We all know or have heard of a sad story of a church or ministry sliding into sin whether it's sexual sin, greed, or some other lust of the flesh. We have allowed the rampant sin that is so blatant in the American culture to become a part of us, the church. This should not be and God desires for His people to praise and worship Him all the days of our lives and to live as "*more than conquerors*" because of His love and the blood of His Son.

This book will address worship and adoration first. The only way to adore God is to have a desire to be less of yourself and more of Him. Humans are naturally self-involved and as long as you are the most important person in your life you have taken Jesus off the throne and sat down in His place. Let the convicting

> § A worshiper without warring will seldom see victory and a warrior who does not worship will lose sight of Who is on the throne.

> § You must desire less of you and more of Him.

power of the Holy Spirit make this a life changing experience so that you will get to hear *"Well done, good and faithful servant"* and see God smile.

Prayer - Father, I desire to love You and adore You. I ask that You show me and lead me by Your Holy Spirit to learn to worship You so that I can say with everything that is within me, 'Lord, I have loved the habitation of Your house and the place where Your glory dwells'. Make this a reality in me. Let me see and feel Your glory, in Jesus' name, Amen.

Chapter 1

PURPOSE IN YOUR HEART

Genesis 1:1 *"In the beginning God created the heavens and earth."*

The verses following in the first chapter of Genesis describe the orderly creation completed by the Creator of the heavens and the earth. God is a God of order and He is very detail oriented. This chapter tells of one miracle after another. *"The Spirit of God was hovering over the face of the waters."* Then God spoke and there was light, and He separated the light from the dark. God made the firmament and divided the waters and called the firmament heaven. On the third day He gathered the waters together and made dry land. The dry land became earth and the waters He called the seas. On the same day God made the vegetation that covered the earth. On the fourth day God put the light in the heavens. He created the sun and the moon so that there would be day and night and He made the seasons and signs for days and years. On the fifth day God made the creatures in the sea and the birds of the air. On the sixth day He made every living creature on the earth and then He made man in His image according to His likeness. By the end of the sixth day God made man and woman and then He blessed them and said, *"Be fruitful and multiply; fill the earth and subdue it; have dominion over the fish of the sea, over the birds of the air, and over every living thing that moves on the earth".* (Genesis 1:28)

After each day of creation God always saw that it was good. He was pleased with His creation and then He rested on the seventh day and blessed all the work of His hands and declared it to be good.

Even though we have earthly fathers our true Father is the God of the heavens and the earth. God is the one who knew us before the beginning of the world. Ephesians 1:3, 4 says, *"Blessed be the God and Father of our Lord Jesus Christ, Who has blessed us with every spiritual blessing in the heavenly places in Christ, just as He chose us in Him before the foundation of the world."* Also, in Jeremiah 1:5 the Lord spoke to Jeremiah, saying, *"Before I formed you in the womb I knew you."* Our Father knew us. He formed us. He gave us life. The same God that made all of creation made you and me. He made us. He fashioned us. He is so vast and magnificent yet also so intimate to

§
Creation was not an accident but was a purposeful act by our Creator.

§
He knew you before the foundation of the world and He formed you in your mother's womb.

care about us and look down from the heavens and give us life. The magnificence of God is framed by the crashing of the sea and awesome expanse of the glorious mountains that seem to stretch to the heavens.

Psalm 95:1-7 says:

> *"Oh come, let us sing to the LORD!*
> *Let us shout joyfully to the Rock of our salvation.*
> *Let us come before His presence with thanksgiving;*
> *let us shout joyfully to Him with psalms.*
> *For the LORD is the great God,*
> *and the great King above all gods.*
> *In His hand are the deep places of the earth;*
> *the heights of the hills are His also.*
> *The sea is His, for He made it;*
> *and His hands formed the dry land.*
> *Oh come, let us worship and bow down;*
> *let us kneel before the LORD our Maker.*
> *For He is our God,*
> *and we are the people of His pasture,*
> *and the sheep of His hand."*

§ Ask God to give you a hunger to worship Him.

If you have never experienced worship that takes you out of yourself and into the throne room of God, then ask God to give you a hunger to worship Him.

Prayer - Oh Father, I ask that You put in me a heart to worship and adore You. Place such a deep hunger in me for a love relationship with You that I long to be in Your presence. Let me feel Your presence, hear Your voice, seek Your face, and touch Your heart. Take me past me and into Your place of worship and glory, in Jesus' name, Amen.

Renee Vetter

1. Who is God that I should worship Him? Write your thoughts and use scripture.

2. Find a scripture that speaks of worshiping God that was not in this chapter and purpose in your heart to memorize it. Write it down.

3. What do you sense that God is speaking to you through this chapter and the time that you have spent with Him?

4. Have you allowed your heart to grow cold to worship, or have you never experienced it before? Write down your answer from your heart to God's heart. It is time to be real and vulnerable to God who knows all about you anyway. Get real with Him. Cry out to be a man or woman of worship!

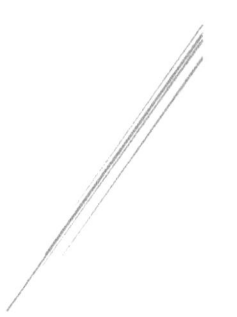

"YES, I HAVE LOVED YOU WITH AN EVERLASTING LOVE"

Jeremiah 31:3b, *"Yes, I have loved you with an everlasting love; therefore with loving-kindness have I drawn you and continued My faithfulness to you."* AMPC

Does God know us personally and love us individually? Does He know my strengths and weaknesses? Does He love me in spite of my inadequacies? Read this psalm of David.

> Psalm 139:13-16
> *"For You formed my inward parts;*
> *You covered me in my mother's womb.*
> *I will praise You, for I am fearfully and wonderfully made;*
> *marvelous are Your works,*
> *and that my soul knows very well.*
> *My frame was not hidden from You,*
> *when I was made in secret,*
> *and skillfully wrought in the lowest parts of the earth.*
> *Your eyes saw my substance, being yet unformed.*
> *and in Your book they all were written,*
> *the days fashioned for me,*
> *when as yet there were none of them."*

David was called a man after God's own heart. There are many verses in the Bible which show that God knew us, fashioned us, and loved us before the beginning of the world. God calls us the apple of His eye in Psalm 17:8. In John 3:16 we read that God so loved the world that He gave His most precious gift, His son Jesus.

Jeremiah 1:5, *"Before I formed you in the womb I knew you; before you were born I sanctified you; I ordained you a prophet to the nations."*

Jeremiah was just a youth when he was called by God to bring a message of impending doom to His people because of their wickedness and corruption. Since God does not show favoritism as Peter said in Act 10:34, and if God knew David and Jeremiah, He also knows us.

Jeremiah 29:11 *"For I know the plans I have for you,"* declares the LORD, *"plans to prosper you and not to harm you, plans to give you hope and a future."* NIV

§
God loves me even when I fall short.

God knows the plans that He has for us, plans to prosper us, not harm us. Plans to give us hope and a future. Another translation says plans for good and not for evil. God knew us before He formed us in our mother's womb. He breathed life into us. God loves us and He loves us unconditionally, even when we fail.

God called David a man after His own heart yet David was not perfect, he was a man with a past. But David had a repentant heart. After David had sinned with Bathsheba the Lord sent Nathan to him. In 2 Samuel chapter twelve, the story unfolds and David is sent correction from God through His prophet Nathan. In verse thirteen David answers Nathan by saying *"I have sinned against the Lord."*

> § He loves us in spite of our sin.

David's sin was forgiven and his second son by Bathsheba, Solomon, succeeded him to the throne just before David's death. Bathsheba and David's first son, who was conceived when she was married to Uriah, died. Even though David sinned with Bathsheba and sent her husband to be killed in the front lines of the battle, he repented immediately when God sent Nathan the prophet to him. David was not perfect but he loved God and his heart was tender towards God and the things of God. David sinned greatly against God and all the people involved in this sordid mess. But David cried out and was forgiven because he had a repentant heart. There were consequences for this sin however, and David lost two sons and his daughter was raped by her brother. Sounds like a mess because it was a mess. But God in His mercy and wisdom saw David's heart and ordained that Jesus would come from the bloodline of David. In Mathew 1:1 Jesus is called the Son of David.

Before the Lord formed us He knew us. He doesn't love us because we have never sinned. He loves us in spite of our sin. Realize that God loves you and has wonderful plans for your life, for good and not for evil. He loves you because God is love and you are a child of His if you have trusted Jesus as your Savior. God is your Father and He loves you as a father loves his child. In some cases, our fathers have harmed us, so do not put the face of an abusive father on the face of a loving and perfect God.

God loves us, He knew us before the beginning of the world and He has fashioned us for a good purpose. Our pasts are forgiven as soon as we ask and our hope is in Christ *"the author and finisher of our faith"*.

Prayer - Father, I thank You that You love me and that You knew me even before I drew a breath. Thank You that You have a purpose for my life and that You desire to use me in Your kingdom. I thank You God that Your plans for my life are for good and not evil and I ask You Father to reveal to me the plans for my life and give me a desire to walk out my destiny for Your glory, in Jesus' name, Amen.

1. Find another character besides Jeremiah and David in the Bible that could also be used as an example. Write out the verse or verses. One example is Esther, but there are many more.

2. Does God love me, just as I am? How do I know that? Use scripture.

3. Do you know the plans God has for you? If so, write them down and what God has told you about those plans. If not, ask Him now and record what you sense is His answer.

PURPOSE IN YOUR HEART TO BE A RECEIVER FROM GOD AND BELIEVE HIS WORD

John 1:1-4, 14 "*In the beginning was the Word, and the Word was with God, and the Word was God. He was in the beginning with God. All things were made through Him, and without Him nothing was made that was made. In Him was life, and the life was the light of men."* 14 *"And the Word became flesh and dwelt among us, and we beheld His glory, the glory as of the only begotten of the Father, full of grace and truth."*

God not only loves us because we are His creation, He loved us enough to send His only son Jesus to walk the earth as a man, a sinless man, yet a man. God made a way for us to be reconciled to Himself once and for all. He did that through the death, burial and resurrection of His Son. The only way that sins were forgiven under the old covenant was through a blood sacrifice. The priests would sacrifice animals and the blood would atone for the sins of their people. But God had a new and better way.

§
God sent His Son because He loves us.

Philippians 2:5-8 "*Let this mind be in you which was also in Christ Jesus, Who, being in the form of God, did not consider it robbery to be equal with God, but made Himself of no reputation, taking the form of a bondservant, and coming in the likeness of men. And being found in appearance as a man, He humbled Himself and became obedient to the point of death, even the death of the cross."*

Jesus was equal to God, yet came to the earth and became a man. He did this in order to satisfy the requirements once and for all to atone for man's fall to sin. He made it possible for us to walk with God in the cool of the day as Adam and Eve did prior to their fall to sin, to be filled with His presence and be a child of His once again. Why would God send His son? Because, *"God so loved the world that He sent His only begotten Son so that whoever believes in Him should not perish but have everlasting life."* (John 3:16)

Ephesians 2:4 -10 *"But God, who is rich in mercy, because of His great love with which He loved us, even when we were dead in trespasses, made us alive together with Christ (by grace you have been saved), and raised us up together, and made us sit together in the heavenly places in Christ Jesus, that in the ages to come He might show the exceeding riches of His grace in His kindness toward us in Christ Jesus. For by grace you have been saved through faith,*

and that not of yourselves; it is the gift of God, not of works, lest anyone should boast. For we are His workmanship, created in Christ Jesus for good works, which God prepared beforehand that we should walk in them."

God sent His Son because God is rich in mercy and grace and He loves us with a love that is not of this world. God loves us with a perfect love, not a human love. We were dead in sin but through salvation we are now made alive and not only alive but we are in a place of power and authority. We are seated with Christ Jesus in heavenly places. Jesus is at the right hand of the Father, as are we, because we are seated with Him. Read Ephesians 1:20 and chapter two, verse six.

God's grace is what has saved us through faith in Jesus and acceptance of Him as our Savior. God's grace is unmerited favor, a gift from Him to us. Jesus came *"that they may have life, and that they may have it more abundantly."* (John 10:10b) Jesus came to reconcile us unto the Father once and for all, and to restore our heavenly citizenship with the power, authority, and blessings of royalty. Satan is the one who wants to keep us in poverty and enslave us to sin. He is the one who wants to abuse us and even kill us. In John 10:10a, the Bible says, *"The thief does not come except to steal, and to kill, and to destroy."* The devil is the destroyer but Jesus is the Restorer. Hallelujah!

Jesus came to put us in right standing with God not just for when we die, but also as we walk out this life. John 14, in verses twelve through fourteen the Bible says, *"Most assuredly, I say to you, he who believes in Me, the works that I do he will do also; and greater works than these he will do, because I go to My Father. And whatever you ask in My name, that I will do, that the Father may be glorified in the Son. If you ask anything in My name, I will do it."*

Understand that Jesus not only made a way for us to enter heaven He also made a way for us to rule on the earth with power and authority, washed in His blood, filled with His Spirit, and clothed with the armor of God.

"For we are His workmanship, created in Christ Jesus for good works, which God prepared beforehand that we should walk in them."(Ephesians 2:10) God has so much that He wants to give us. But because of fear, laziness, disbelief or possibly incorrect teaching, far too many times we settle for much less than what He has for us. Whatever it is that holds us back from

> §
> The devil is the destroyer, but Jesus is the Restorer!

experiencing more of God, we need to recognize it and ask for forgiveness for that sin and determine to believe God and to believe His Word.

God has tipped the scales and the only way we can refuse Him is to refuse His gift, Jesus Christ. The only way we can refuse a walk of victory and power is to refuse to accept **all** of His Word. We are washed in the blood and we are filled with the Holy Spirit so that we can truly become more than conquerors. God's job is to give, ours is to receive. Purpose in your heart to be a receiver.

Prayer - Teach me, Father, to be bold, to ask and believe that I will receive a blessing from You. Begin to work in me a victorious heart which prepares for success and does not settle for less than Your best. Give me a heart to believe Your Word, all of Your Word, not just parts. Place within me a receptive heart, listening ears, and a discerning spirit, so that I may follow You all the days of my life. Show me how to be a believer and a receiver, in Jesus' name I pray, Amen.

§
Jesus came to give you life AND an abundant life!

1. What do you sense God is saying to you through this lesson? Write your answer and refer to the scriptures that speak to you most. Find another scripture that explains why God needed to send Jesus for us. Write it down and memorize it.

2. Who is Jesus and who is He to you? Use scripture.

3. Are you blocking your receiving from God? If so, in what way? Do you feel unworthy or are you full of fear? Maybe you are just lazy and don't want to get into the Word of God and be changed. Is it possible you are believing in the traditions of men instead of the living Word of God?

GOD'S WORD IS A TOTAL PACKAGE

John 16:7 *"However, I am telling you nothing but the truth when I say it is profitable (good, expedient, advantageous) for you that I go away. Because if I do not go away, the Comforter (Counselor, Helper, Advocate, Intercessor, Strengthener, Standby) will not come to you [into close fellowship with you] but if I go away, I will send Him to you [to be in close fellowship with you]."* AMPC

Just before Jesus ascended into heaven, He told His followers not to leave Jerusalem but to wait for what the Father had promised them. Acts 1:1-9 gives the account of Jesus explaining to them one last time before He ascended to wait, be baptized, receive power, and be witnesses for Him. This is not a water baptism but a baptism with the Holy Spirit.

John 16:7 was Jesus' very own words. He said that it would be advantageous for us when He left, because we would have the Holy Spirit to be our Comforter, Counselor, Helper, Advocate, Intercessor, Strengthener, and Standby. Being baptized with the Holy Spirit does not mean you get more Holy Spirit. When you were born again you were sealed with the Holy Spirit as the Word states in Ephesians 4:30. When you are filled with the Holy Spirit, He gets more of you. This allows you to have a greater sensitivity to God's voice as well as operate in the gifts of the Holy Spirit which I will discuss later in this chapter.

This is a Bible study, therefore those who read this are seeking a closer relationship with God, or more knowledge of His Word. This person's desire is typically to change their life in some way. I can give you knowledge or teach you but what we all need is the saving knowledge of Jesus Christ and the understanding of the total surrender to the Holy Spirit. This is a Bible study on prayer and spiritual warfare designed to give you knowledge of God's Word and a hunger for a move of the Holy Spirit that changes your world.

Do not allow the traditions of men or even your denominational views to rob you of the Word of God. Some denominations teach that the gifts of the Holy Spirit were only for the first church. If this were true then the Holy Spirit died with the first church. To the other extreme, there are denominations that teach if you do not speak in tongues, you are not saved. Both of these are lies and reveal an ignorance of God's Word. The Bible does not teach that the Holy Spirit died and if the Holy Spirit is alive and active, there are gifts explained in 1st Corinthians the twelfth chapter that God wants us to operate in.

> §
> Do not allow the traditions of men or even your denominational views to rob you of the Word of God.

We are not to deny the power of the Holy Spirit nor call His gifts dead. It is time for the church to arise and be the victorious church that God wants us to be. Jesus came so that we *"may have life and have it more abundantly."* He sent back the Holy Spirit so that we could fulfill the great commission which is more than spreading the gospel. Matthew 10:7-8 says, "*And as you go, preach, saying, 'The kingdom of heaven is at hand.' Heal the sick, cleanse the lepers, raise the dead, cast out demons. Freely you have received, freely give.*"

> §
> We need to act like kingdom people and live like kingdom people who operate in the power by the Holy Spirit.

When we get saved the Holy Spirit takes up residence in our spirit but when we are baptized with the Holy Spirit, we do not get more of Him, He gets more of us. So we are immersed in the *"rivers of living water"* as it says in John 7:38. We have to get past man's doctrine and believe the whole gospel and not just the portions that we feel comfortable with. Jesus did not come to make us comfortable. He came so that we could be changed into His image and do the works that He did, as well as to reconcile us once and for all to the Father.

I am not down playing what Jesus did. I am agreeing with Him that the kingdom of heaven is here. So we need to act like kingdom people and live like kingdom people who operate in power by the Holy Spirit.

1 Corinthians 12:4-11 "*There are diversities of gifts, but the same Spirit. There are differences of ministries, but the same Lord. And there are diversities of activities, but it is the same God who works all in all. But the manifestation of the Spirit is given to each one for the profit of all: for to one is given the word of wisdom through the Spirit, to another the word of knowledge through the same Spirit, to another faith by the same Spirit, to another gifts of healings by the same Spirit, to another the working of miracles, to another prophecy, to another discerning of spirits, to another different kinds of tongues, to another the interpretation of tongues. But one and the same Spirit works all these things, distributing to each one individually as He wills.*"

Malachi 3:6 *"For I am the LORD, I do not change;"*

God does not change. We are the same church as the first church and we are to function just as the first church. Man's doctrine has taken the power from the church to change our world for Christ. We are to be believers not scoffers. We cannot out-think God and presume that God has changed His mind. We are not to be trapped by man's

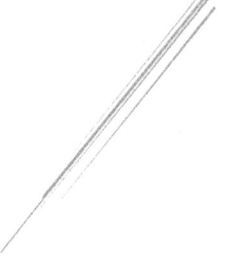

theology and what we think God said. God does not change so if He poured out His Holy Spirit and He came with gifts, then so be it. Don't allow man's tradition or doctrine to rob you of a life filled with the power of God which will change your life and those around you.

Jesus said in Matthew 10:7-9 that we are to spread the gospel, heal the sick, raise the dead and cast out demons. Spreading the gospel is one out of four commands. If we did just 25% of our jobs in the secular world we'd be fired. The truth is we are to be baptized with the Holy Spirit after we are saved. This is a different experience. The truth is the gifts are still for the church as the Spirit wills for the good of the body. The truth is we are to be worshiping in power, walking in power, and spreading the gospel. Accompanying signs will follow us: healing the sick, raising the dead and casting out demons. God's Word is a total package or He would not have saved it for us. Do not turn away from the whole Word of God. Embrace it.

I have already walked as a powerless Christian, and I refuse to go back to that place again *"having a form of godliness but denying its power."* (2 Timothy 3:5) I need to have the power of the Holy Spirit operating in me all the time, do you?

Prayer - I ask You, Father, to fill me with the Holy Spirit and I surrender all of me to be filled with all of Your Holy Spirit. I surrender totally and I receive Him now. I thank You that I also receive the gifts of the Holy Spirit because they come with this complete surrender and infilling of the Holy Spirit.

> §
> Do not turn away from the whole Word of God. Embrace it.

1. Does the power of the Holy Spirit work through you? If not, why not?

2. What scripture impacted you the most in this lesson?

3. Who is the Holy Spirit and who is He to you? Use scripture.

4. What must you do to change your life from being powerless to being power filled by the Holy Spirit?

5. What is the Holy Spirit telling you about your faith level, belief level and obedience level?

Chapter 2

THE LORD WILL NOT SHARE HIS THRONE WITH ANOTHER

Genesis 2:16-17 *"Of every tree of the garden you may freely eat; but of the tree of the knowledge of good and evil you shall not eat, for in the day that you eat of it you shall surely die."*

Genesis 3:1-5 *"Now the serpent was more cunning than any beast of the field which the LORD God had made. And he said to the woman, "Has God indeed said, 'You shall not eat of every tree of the garden'?" And the woman said to the serpent, "We may eat the fruit of the trees of the garden; but of the fruit of the tree which is in the midst of the garden, God has said, 'You shall not eat it, nor shall you touch it, lest you die.' "Then the serpent said to the woman, "You will not surely die. For God knows that in the day you eat of it your eyes will be opened and you will be like God, knowing good and evil."*

§
Who is on the throne?

God told Adam and Eve not to eat of the tree of knowledge of good and evil. John 8:44 tells us that the devil is a liar and has lied to us from the beginning. Sin came into the world when Eve was deceived and Adam fell with her into temptation. It was the pride of life that dropped over their eyes and from that day forward man has been born with a sin nature. We needed a Savior, someone who would be that perfect sacrifice once and for all to save us from our sin. That Savior was Jesus and He bore our sin on the cross, was crucified and rose again so that through Christ we could receive new life. Jesus was our sin offering. We have been set free from sin and death. However, the enemy is still here on earth with us. In his instructions on being submissive to God but resisting the devil, Peter said, *"Be sober; be vigilant, because your adversary the devil walks about like a roaring lion, seeking whom he may devour."* (1 Peter 5:8) The devil is our enemy and he has come to destroy us. Jesus said, *"The thief (the devil) does not come except to steal, and to kill, and to destroy."* (John 10:10a)

The Word is very clear about the devil, about who he is and his works. He is roaming about the earth seeking to devour us. According to Webster's Dictionary, devour means to destroy or consume with violence. The Lord is telling us that we have a personal enemy who's

out to consume us, steal from us or kill us. That is his goal. For some reason, it is easy for us to believe that Jesus is a personal Savior, but not that the devil is a personal destroyer.

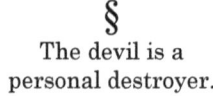
The devil is a personal destroyer.

We have been taught in the majority of our churches that the devil cannot touch us or that his power is so minimal that he is a buffoon. He is something or someone to be laughed at like the boogey man. If that were true, then why didn't Jesus, the Son of God, laugh at the devil in the wilderness? Jesus knew who the devil was and He did not foolishly disregard him. Jesus answered him soberly and spoke back to him the Word of God. As previously noted, first Peter tells us that we are to be sober and vigilant which means watchful and alert, even cautious. The book of first Peter was written to the church which means the Lord wants the church, that's us, to be sober, watchful, and alert because the devil is a roaming and roaring lion seeking whom he may devour. In other words, the devil is always on the move and his goal is to destroy you. The devil is also called the father of lies and he will reveal himself to you, but he will try to hide from you that he is the destroyer. He's crafty and he will subtly, rather than obviously, come against what the Lord has told you or come against His Word.

The Bible also states in Ephesians 2:2 that the devil is called the prince of the power of the air. In 2 Thessalonians 2:8 the devil is called the lawless one. He comes in different forms but his purpose is always the same: to steal, kill and destroy. (John 10:10)

Isaiah tells of the devil being cast to the ground by God.

Isaiah 14:12-14 *"How you are fallen from heaven, O Lucifer, son of the morning! How you are cut down to the ground, you who weakened the nations! For you have said in your heart: 'I will ascend into heaven, I will exalt my throne above the stars of God; I will also sit on the mount of the congregation on the farthest sides of the north; I will ascend above the heights of the clouds, I will be like the Most High.'"*

for power and the right to do what he wanted to do, when and how he wanted to do it and he wanted to control others. Lucifer said "I will" five times in the verses above. He was a being created by God and he lusted to be higher than the One who created him. He rebelled against God, and it is that same rebellion that he planted in man when Adam and Eve went into sin by disobeying God. Satan was an anointed cherub full of wisdom and perfect in beauty. Satan, also known as Lucifer, wanted to rule his own life and all those he came in contact with. He aspired to take God's place and rule over all the heavens and the earth. He lusted

Read the following verses:

Ezekiel 28:12b-17 *"You were the seal of perfection, full of wisdom and perfect in beauty. You were in Eden, the garden of God; every precious stone was your covering: The sardius, topaz, and diamond, beryl, onyx, and jasper, sapphire, turquoise, and emerald with gold. The workmanship of your timbrels and pipes was prepared for you on the day you were created. You were the anointed cherub who covers; I established you; you were on the holy mountain of God; you walked back and forth in the midst of fiery stones. You were perfect in your ways from the day you were created, till iniquity was found in you. By the abundance of your trading you became filled with violence within, and you sinned; therefore I cast you as a profane thing out of the mountain of God; and I destroyed you, O covering cherub, from the midst of the fiery stones. Your heart was lifted up because of your beauty; you corrupted your wisdom for the sake of your splendor; I cast you to the ground,"*

§ The devil wanted to be like God.

God said that Lucifer was perfect in his ways from the day he was created until iniquity, or wickedness was found in him. Verse seventeen states that the pride of his beauty and wisdom corrupted him and he rebelled against God. He began to exalt himself above God. The Lord will not share His throne with another. The creation is never greater than the Creator. Satan became prideful and then designed a plan to place himself above God. That is what happens when arrogance and haughtiness (pride) consume you. He rebelled and as a result of his rebellion he was cast to the ground. That is where man is, on the ground or the earth. God created us, loved us, and warned us not to fall into pride, because He knew that would separate us from Him. It would also leave us vulnerable to the devil and his schemes.

Adam and Eve rebelled against what God had told them. God said do not and they did anyway. That is rebellion. We were created to walk in the garden with God. Temptation does come and we are to do what Jesus did in the desert when he was tempted. *"Now when the tempter came to Him, he said, 'If You are the Son of God, command that these stones become bread.' But He answered and said, 'It is written, 'Man shall not live by bread alone, but by every word that proceeds from the mouth of God' ".* (Matthew 4:4) Jesus wielded the Word like a sword and destroyed the temptation with the Word. *"...the sword of the Spirit, which is the word of God".* (Ephesians 6:17) We, too, are to take the Word of God to defeat the enemy. However, many of us do not even realize that the devil is even

§
You must understand the traps of the enemy.

speaking to us and we do not know how to stop it. You must first recognize you are under attack. Then you must stop the attacks with the Word which is the sword of the Spirit. Speak scripture, God's Word, back to Satan.

Isaiah 55:11 *"So shall My word be that goes forth from My mouth; it shall not return to Me void, but it shall accomplish what I please, and it shall prosper in the thing for which I sent it."*

The Word is powerful and it will accomplish what God wants it to accomplish. Do not diminish the power of the devil but do not exalt it either. We have the name of Jesus, the Word and the blood of Jesus, which are the most powerful weapons ever created. We will discuss these more in later chapters.

Prayer - Oh God, let me see the enemy for who he is and let me not be afraid but teach me Your Word so that I can be more than a conqueror. Let me see warfare through the eyes of a warrior and the heart of a worshiper.

1. Who is the enemy? Use scripture to prove it.

2. What has the devil done to mankind? Use scripture.

3. What should our attitude be towards the devil?

4. What are our weapons? Use scripture.

"BUT WHY DO YOU CALL ME 'LORD, LORD,' AND DO NOT DO THE THINGS WHICH I SAY?"

John 3:16-17 "*For God so loved the world that He gave His only begotten Son, that whoever believes in Him should not perish but have everlasting life. For God did not send His Son into the world to condemn the world, but that the world through Him might be saved.*"

Matthew 18:11 "*For the Son of Man has come to save that which was lost.*"

Jesus came to save the lost. He came to give us eternal life through salvation. That is a born again experience. The only way to the Father is through the Son. Jesus came so that we might live with Him throughout eternity.

In First Timothy 2:4, the Word says Jesus *"desires all men to be saved and to come to the knowledge of the truth."*

God gave His Son for the whole world to be saved. He desires all men to be saved but unfortunately, not all men will be saved. Man's will is involved and many have not chosen, nor will choose Jesus Christ as their Savior. First Corinthians 1:18 states *"the message of the cross is foolishness to those who are perishing, but to us who are being saved it is the power of God."* Jesus, who is the Son of God, came to earth as a man to live and die for us so that we might live and die with Him. Once our time here is over, we will live eternally with God because we have been redeemed by the blood of the cross. "*We are confident, yes, well pleased rather to be absent from the body and to be present with the Lord.*" (2 Corinthians 5:8)

Ephesians 2:4-9 "*But God, who is rich in mercy, because of His great love with which He loved us, even when we were dead in trespasses, made us alive together with Christ (by grace you have been saved), and raised us up together, and made us sit together in the heavenly places in Christ Jesus, that in the ages to come He might show the exceeding riches of His grace in His kindness toward us in Christ Jesus. For by grace you have been saved through faith, and that not of yourselves; it is the gift of God, not of works, lest anyone should boast.*"

God is rich in mercy and He made a way for us so that we could be with Him forever and ever. There is nothing we can do to earn this. This is a gift that comes only through faith in His Son Jesus. This is a gift to us and it is not because we deserve it or have earned it but because of God's mercy and His grace.

§
God is rich in mercy and He has made a way for us

Jesus died and rose again through the resurrection power of God. Jesus' death on the cross saved us but He did not stop there. *"I have come that they may have life, and that they may have it more abundantly."* (John 10:10b) Jesus came to give us life and life more abundantly. Many times, we are satisfied to stop at salvation but because Jesus died for us, we will live eternally. Because He rose, we have the opportunity to live an abundant life on this earth, filled with the Holy Spirit and operating in the gifts of the Holy Spirit as the Spirit wills for the good of others.

We are to have life and have it more abundantly. That isn't talking about heaven, it's talking about here and now. We go from the kingdom of darkness as sinners to the kingdom of His dear Son when we are saved. Therefore, we become children of God and we are able to receive the blessings from God because we now belong to Him.

> §
> The truth is God's Word, His Son and His Holy Spirit.

In my own case I had to walk away from friends and I angered my family because my life was now not my own. I made some mistakes because I was so excited about Jesus and this new life within me, but I was just different. I no longer drank, cursed, or any of the other things I did in the world. I was radically saved and I radically made people angry because of this change. I learned quickly to adapt my life to God's plan for my life.

John 14:12-14 *"I tell you the truth, anyone who believes in me will do the same works I have done, and even greater works, because I am going to be with the Father. You can ask for anything in my name, and I will do it, so that the Son can bring glory to the Father. Yes, ask me for anything in my name, and I will do it!"* NLT

After Jesus spoke these words to His disciples, He goes on to describe the Holy Spirit. He then explains that after He has gone to be with the Father, the Lord will send the Holy Spirit to us. We need the Holy Spirit so that we can do the same miracles that Jesus has done and even greater ones because He is with the Father. Read what He said in John 14:12-14 again. We just have to ask the Father in the name of the Son. Please don't allow yourself to be trapped in man's tradition which will steal the power from God's Word, deny His Spirit, and steal away from you the destiny that God has for you.

John 4:23-24 *"But the hour is coming, and now is, when the true worshipers will worship the Father in spirit and truth; for the Father is seeking such to worship Him. God is Spirit, and those who worship Him must worship in spirit and truth."*

The truth is God's Word, His Son and His Holy Spirit. We do not get to pick what we like and leave the rest. God's whole Word is true and it is for today as much as it was for two thousand years ago. When we accept God's Word as truth then we will begin to understand what true worship is and what it isn't. Worship isn't just a song and a feeling. It is also knowledge of Who God is and what He promises us as His children.

These are perilous times and sin is being exalted and purity is being scorned in all types of media. We need the power of the Holy Spirit to counteract the wickedness of this time where we have become so accepting of the perversions of sin and call them normal and yet call the godly dangerous.

Prayer - Dear Father, I ask that You work in me a willing and obedient heart that trusts You and Your Word; not my interpretation of Your Word, but Your Word. I ask that You make me a believer who will go forth and preach the gospel, heal the sick, raise the dead and cast out demons, in Jesus' name, Amen.

1. What did Jesus do on the Cross?

2. What does the empty tomb signify to you? Use scriptures.

3. What abilities have been given to believers?

BE A BELIEVER AND SET THE CAPTIVES FREE

Matthew 16:19 *"And I will give you the keys of the kingdom of heaven, and whatever you bind on earth will be bound in heaven, and whatever you loose on earth will be loosed in heaven."*

§

Matthew 10:7-8 *"And as you go, preach, saying, 'The kingdom of heaven is at hand.' "Heal the sick, cleanse the lepers, raise the dead, cast out demons."*

Jesus has passed on to His church the keys (the authority or control) to bind a demon and loose someone from the devil's grasp. Jesus has passed that authority on to His church because the kingdom of heaven has come. In Luke 10:19 Jesus gives the authority over demons to His disciples.

Luke 10:19 *"Behold, I give you the authority to trample on serpents and scorpions, and over all the power of the enemy, and nothing shall by any means hurt you."*

The cross is the place of surrender but the empty tomb is the place of power. Without the cross there is no empty tomb. Without the empty tomb there is eternal life, but no power of the Holy Spirit to fill us, use us, and work signs and wonders through us. The cross has given us life and life everlasting but the power of the resurrection has given us the grace, or ability, to walk in power all of our days.

§

Be a Believer. That's what believers do!

We discussed previously that Jesus has told us to preach the gospel, heal the sick, raise the dead and cast out demons. In these verses in Matthew and in Luke, Jesus has given us the keys to the kingdom and the authority to trample on serpents and scorpions. These terms refer to demons. Jesus said that He has given us authority over the power of the enemy.

In Matthew 12, the Pharisees heard about Jesus casting out demons and they said that He was doing that in the power of the devil. Jesus answered them and said, *"But if I cast out demons by the Spirit of God, surely the kingdom of God has come upon you. Or how can one enter a strong man's house and plunder his goods, unless he first binds the strong man? And then he will plunder his house."* (Matthew 12:28-29)

The Pharisees, who are the men caught up in religion instead of a relationship with Christ, will always call a move of God the move of the devil instead. Otherwise they will have to admit that they are in love with rules and regulations and not a living Lord. Jesus explained to them that a house divided will not stand and Satan cannot cast out Satan. Then He goes on to say that you must first bind a strong man before you can plunder his house.

Remember what you bind on the earth will be bound in heaven and what you loose on the earth will be loosed in heaven. Jesus passed on

to us that authority and those keys by the blood of the cross. In Greek this really means what is bound in heaven will be bound on earth and what is loosed in heaven will be loosed on earth. God has a desire for us and that desire is for us to be saved, set free, and fulfilling the call on our lives until our days are over or until Jesus comes for us.

Matthew 18:18 *"Assuredly, I say to you, whatever you bind on earth will be bound in heaven, and whatever you loose on earth will be loosed in heaven."*

Ephesians 3:19-20 *"to know the love of Christ, which passes knowledge; that you may be filled with all the fullness of God. Now to Him who is able to do exceedingly abundantly above all that we ask or think, according to the power that works in us."*

§
What you bind on earth will be bound in heaven and what you loose on earth will be loosed in heaven.

What powerful verses those are. They are not just words, they are truth. We are to ask to know the love of Christ. Jesus loved us so much that He lived and died and lived again for us. He walked the earth as man yet He was God. He lived in the fullness of God and we are to live that way as well. When we are filled with the Holy Spirit and desiring to walk in the realm where the supernatural is natural, then we are walking in the fullness of God. We have no power in our flesh to change ourselves more or less than anyone else, but in the power of the Holy Spirit we have the fullness of God. What can God do with someone who walks in the fullness of Him?

§
When we are filled with the Holy Spirit and desiring to walk in the realm where the supernatural is natural, then we are walking in the fullness of God.

Ephesians 3:20 *"Now to Him who is able to do exceedingly abundantly above all that we ask or think, according to the power that works in us."*

This is what God can do: He can do exceedingly abundantly **above** all that we ask or think. The next phrase is also very important. *"According to the power that works in us."* So if we are powerless, then guess what? God will do very little through us. We are to spread the gospel, cast out demons, heal the sick, and raise the dead by the power of the Holy Spirit. Determine in your heart to be a God seeker and be ever filled with the Holy Spirit. I want God to do exceedingly abundantly **above** all that I ask or think in a mighty way. So I want all that God has for me and I desire to be used to change this world forever. Be a believer and set the captives free.

Many Christians teach that if you sit under the Word of God long enough you will be set free of demons. Jesus was named the Word and He cast out demons. The former is not only faulty logic it is also faulty scripturally. You cannot memorize enough scriptures or do enough Bible studies to walk in the fullness of God's Spirit. You must *"be filled with the fullness of God."* Believe and walk in His Word.

Prayer - God, make me a believer of Your Word. Put Your Word in my heart and mouth and let me be a God seeker, a God pleaser and a Holy Spirit filled kingdom walker who believes, in Jesus' name, Amen.

1. Do you have the right to cast out demons? Use scripture.

2. What are the keys to the kingdom?

3. Do you desire to be a kingdom walker? What do you have to change in order to line yourself up with God?

OBEDIENCE IS SPIRITUAL WARFARE

1 Samuel 15:22 *"So Samuel said: "Has the Lord as great delight in burnt offerings and sacrifices, as in obeying the voice of the Lord? Behold, to obey is better than sacrifice, and to heed than the fat of rams."*

How do we obey God? Do we obey His word or do we only open our Bible on Sunday? Do we get all our information from our pastor or favorite TV preacher? If that is the case, we only know what they believe. We repeat what men say preaching and we only know what they believe. We repeat what men say instead of allowing the revelation knowledge of the Word of God to flow through us. We listen and believe in the traditions that have been built by men or their take on what the Word states. We need to search the scriptures daily as exampled by the Bereans in Acts chapter 17. They searched the scriptures to see if what Paul said was true.

§ Acts 17:10, 11 *Then the brethren immediately sent Paul and Silas away by night to Berea. When they arrived, they went into the synagogue of the Jews. These were more fair-minded than those in Thessalonica, in that they received the word with all readiness, and searched the Scriptures daily to find out whether these things were so.*

The church has not been taught much about the enemy. We are told there is an enemy but few teach us about the tactics of the enemy. Then when we get broadsided by the devil many will immediately put God's face on what happened. Some will use one of the pat phrases like: "Well this didn't take God by surprise", or "He is in control so this is to teach me something", or even "It is God's will that this evil happened to me and my family". These are incorrect responses. God does not have children raped so that they will grow up to be men or women of His character. That is an assault by the devil. Nor does the Lord ruin your finances or marriage. Those can be personal choices attributed to bad decision-making processes. Remember, John 10:10a says *"the devil came to kill, steal and destroy"*. What a blessing it would be if church leaders, and churches as a whole, would stop making such ridiculous statements; stop putting the devil's evil acts on the face of God. Put the blame where it goes: on the devil. God is not an abuser and He can fashion the character of His children with love and mercy and compassion.

Now, He **will** turn what was meant for evil into good but He is a holy and pure Father Who loves us and desires us to walk in His ways as we are filled with His Spirit. It is so important that we teach our children that they have an enemy who is seeking to steal, kill and destroy them. We feed our children Biblical fables with talking fruits and vegetables and other characters but we don't teach them about the traps of the enemy. *"Lest Satan should take advantage of us; for we are not ignorant of his devices."* (2 Corinthians 2:11) Unfortunately

> Matthew 10:7 *"And as you go, preach, saying, 'The kingdom of heaven is at hand.'"*

in most cases we are in fact ignorant of Satan and his evil schemes and the result is we never teach our children that we have an enemy, let alone an enemy who is seeking to devour us.

What would happen if we sent our soldiers to war and they never learned anything about fighting the enemy or how to use the weapons given to them? That is exactly what we are doing to ourselves if we don't learn how to combat our enemy. Many Christians think that people are our enemy. Instead, our enemy is the devil and his demons and we must learn to fight.

In order to win a war, we must understand some principles of warfare.

- Who do you serve?
- How do you fight?
- What are your weapons?
- How do they work?
- Who is the enemy?
- How is he defeated?

Jesus defeated the devil with His death on the cross. In the fourth chapter of Ephesians, Paul states that Jesus *"led captive a host of captives"* when He ascended on high. That means that death and hell were conquered by the Lord Jesus Christ but just as we have to receive or appropriate our salvation, we must also receive our deliverance.

> Believer's authority means to take possession or ownership of what Jesus gave us.

The believer's authority means to take possession or ownership of what Jesus gave us. It is as simple as that. We are to spread the gospel but sometimes it is necessary to bind the demons of lying from a person's mind so that they can hear the gospel. In order to pray for someone to be healed many times you must bind off the demon that is causing the disease. In order to raise the dead, you must bind off the demon of death. And in order to cast out demons you must first bind them then cast them out in Jesus' name. We have been given authority by the Lord Jesus Himself to cast out demons, heal the sick and raise the dead. This is our believer's authority.

The Word says that Jesus bore our sickness, disease, iniquities, and transgressions. Many of the people that I work with are basically the walking dead. They have lost all hope because of abuse, addiction, guilt, condemnation, paralyzing flashbacks of abuse or sin, rejection, and the effects of witchcraft that have left dissociative or multiple personality disorders. They don't know how to live abundantly. They are just surviving. Their hope, careers, and destinies are dead and they

need the resurrection power of the Holy Spirit to set them free, heal them, and bring all that was dead back to life. *"Surely He has borne our griefs, and carried our sorrows; Yet we esteemed Him stricken, smitten by God, and afflicted. But He was wounded for our transgressions, He was bruised for our iniquities; the chastisement for our peace was upon Him, And by His stripes we are healed."* (Isaiah 53:4-5)

"Blessed be the LORD my Rock, who trains my hands for war, and my fingers for battle." (Psalm 144:1)

Our first responsibility and desire is to worship God and then we are to do what He has told us to do. **Obedience is spiritual warfare**. King David learned to love and worship God in the sheepfold but he also learned warfare. The Word says that he fought the lion and the bear to save the flock. He was a worshiper and a warrior.

Worship without warfare is not understanding authority. Warfare without worship generates trusting in self. I desire to seek the face of God and I also desire to do the works of the Lord Jesus Christ because I am a believer.

Judges 3:1-4, *"Now these are the nations which the LORD left, that He might test Israel by them, that is, all who had not known any of the wars in Canaan (this was only so that the generations of the children of Israel might be taught to know war, at least those who had not formerly known it), namely, five lords of the Philistines, all the Canaanites, the Sidonians, and the Hivites who dwelt in Mount Lebanon, from Mount Baal Hermon to the entrance of Hamath. And they were left, that He might test Israel by them, to know whether they would obey the commandments of the LORD, which He had commanded their fathers by the hand of Moses."*

God left some of the enemy in order to teach His children warfare and also to test them to see if they would obey His commands. *"God is the same yesterday, today and forever."*

If you have been abused, please do not mix up the works of the devil with the works of God. God does not abuse us, that is the devil, but He does test us to see if we will believe His Word and walk in it. The devil was given free reign over the earth when Adam and Eve fell in the garden and sin entered the world. God made provisions then for them to walk freely and He made provisions for us as well. Those provisions are also weapons: the blood of Jesus, His name and the Word of God.

> § Worship without warfare is not understanding authority.

> § Warfare without worship generates trusting in self.

We have been given authority over the enemy and whether we choose to war or not is up to us. Just because we choose not to war does not make the war go away, it just makes us a casualty unnecessarily because we have the authority to walk in victory as *"more than a conqueror, through Jesus Christ, who loves us."*

Prayer - Father, I ask that You open my understanding and my knowledge of Your Word so that I can be a believer of Your Word. I want the works of Jesus because Jesus said to. He said "greater things will I do than He has done because He goes to be with You". Teach me Your ways, fill me with Your Spirit, and show me how to walk in an atmosphere of faith that will change me and those I come in contact with forever. Make me a believer, and teach me to worship and to war by the power of Your Holy Spirit, in Jesus' name, Amen.

1. What do you need to do to line yourself up with the Word of God? Do you need to remove some sin that is separating you from a closer relationship with the Holy Spirit? Do you need to ask forgiveness for doubt and unbelief? If you do, then command the demons associated with that sin to be gone in Jesus' name.

2. What is the believer's authority?

3. Are you a believer in the Word of God and the power of His might? Use scripture to prove your claim.

Chapter 3

WORSHIP WILL TAKE YOU WHERE KNOWLEDGE CANNOT KEEP YOU

Psalm 27:4

*"One thing I have desired of the LORD,
That will I seek:
That I may dwell in the house of the LORD
All the days of my life,
to behold the beauty of the LORD,
and to inquire in His temple."*

Worship means to desire to spend time in the presence of God. It is not just a brief moment here or there but rather to make staying in His presence a priority and a requirement. Worship is filling your heart with the beauty of His holiness. It is so magnificent that it is hard to describe. In order to worship you must lose who you are in the presence of who He is.

The only way to dwell in the house of the Lord is to dwell in worship and praise, to desire to see His face. Worship is hungering to see a smile cross His lips; to gaze into His face and see love, compassion and mercy pour from His eyes into your soul; to feel the touch of His hand as He places the same hand that made the heavens and the earth against your cheek and wipes away the tears of pain and suffering. Worship is to fall onto your knees in the presence of a holy and awesome God knowing that we deserve death but He has given us life. Worship is connecting your spirit, soul and body to God the Father, Jesus the Son and the Holy Spirit. Worship is to take all of yourself into the presence of all of Him. Worship is drowning in the magnificence of a magnificent God, holding up holy hands and singing with tears flooding from your eyes. Worship is placing your thoughts, your desires and your life at His feet as you kneel before His majesty knowing that you do not deserve to be there but so grateful that the blood of Jesus makes it possible for you. It is the blood that has changed all of us from sinner to forgiven, from bondage to free, and covers us so that as we kneel the likeness of Christ enfolds us and when we hear God say *"Seek My face,"* our hearts say *"Your face Lord, I will seek."* (Psalm 27:8) Worship is a lifestyle of preferring the presence of God to the praises of men. Worship will take you where

§
Worship is to take all of yourself into the presence of all of Him.

§
Worship is the lifestyle of preferring the presence of God to the praises of men.

knowledge cannot keep you. Worship is a condition of the heart and a barometer of the surrender level of all of you to all of Him.

Hebrews 4:16 *"Let us therefore come boldly to the throne of grace that we may obtain mercy and find grace to help in time of need."*

We get to go into the throne room and issue our requests to Him personally. That is where we will find grace and mercy to help when we need help. As you learn to worship and praise the Lord, then you come to understand that God desires to spend time with you. He desires to minister to you, to answer your prayers and to see you and your family walk in wholeness and victory.

James 5:15-18 *"And the prayer of faith will save the sick, and the Lord will raise him up. And if he has committed sins, he will be forgiven. Confess your trespasses to one another, and pray for one another, that you may be healed. The effective, fervent prayer of a righteous man avails much. Elijah was a man with a nature like ours and he prayed earnestly that it would not rain; and it did not rain on the land for three years and six months. And he prayed again, and the heaven gave rain, and the earth produced its fruit."*

Praying with faith, fervency and effectiveness will bring answers from the God who resides within us by His Spirit. As you learn to worship, pray, and do warfare you will see God answer your prayers because He is faithful.

Years ago, I worked with a young boy after having taken his parents through prayers of deliverance. They asked me if I would pray over their seven-year-old son who had autism. He had been perfectly normal until age two and then it all changed. I had never worked with autism before but if he had been normal once then I knew that this had been an attack by the enemy. Remember sickness and disease came into the world when Adam and Eve fell to the lies of the devil in the garden. So when the parents brought the boy to see me I could see in the spirit a helmet around his head that totally cut him off from the world around him. I began to pray over him and then I pulled that helmet off and commanded all demons of isolation and those associated with autism to leave him in the name of Jesus. He looked better but he just sat there and looked at all of us. His mother then took him to lunch on her way to take him back to school. As he walked around the indoor play area, he touched everything as if he had never seen it before. Then

§
Worship is a condition of the heart and a barometer of the surrender level of all of you to all of Him.

§
Praying with faith, fervency and effectiveness will bring answers from the God who resides within us by His Spirit.

§
Proverbs 16:3 *"Roll your works upon the Lord [commit and trust them wholly to Him; He will cause your thoughts to become agreeable to His will, and] so shall your plans be established and succeed."* AMPC

he began to play and show his mom what he could do. He was awakening to his surroundings. God is so faithful. The last time I heard he was coming along well and all I did is walk this out as a true believer.

Psalm 24:3-4

"Who may ascend into the hill of the LORD?
Or who may stand in His holy place?
He who has clean hands and a pure heart,
who has not lifted up his soul to an idol,
nor sworn deceitfully."

Learn to go into His throne room and worship the Father of all creation. When you prepare yourself to go into prayer remember you are going to a holy place and allow God to prepare you.

It is so necessary to check your heart and if you need to ask forgiveness and for cleansing then do so immediately. As you read in the passage from James, sometimes our healing depends on our repentant hearts. Make it your desire to ascend to the throne room and stand in the presence of a holy God. Examine yourself and then begin to thank God for who He is and what He does. Give Him honor in your prayer time. Make sure that to the best of your ability that you have clean hands and a pure heart and that there is no unforgiveness toward others and no personal agenda.

The throne room is a place of intimacy. It is also a place of power. We need to walk in humility filled with the Spirit of God with such a closeness to Him it is as if we can almost feel His breath on our face. Intimacy requires honesty and a complete surrender unto the Lord so that we hear Him when He whispers our name.

2 Corinthians 3:17-18 "*Now the Lord is the Spirit and where the Spirit is, there is liberty. But we all, with unveiled face, beholding in a mirror the glory of the Lord, are being transformed into the same image from glory to glory, just as by the Spirit of the Lord.*"

These two verses are together because they go together. Many people declare they are in liberty without that complete surrender of all of them to all of God. You don't get to hold something back and walk into intimacy with a Holy God. You don't get to live in a fantasy world of romance novels and Lifetime movies and walk in the power of God. Just once, open your heart and let all of the secret places be open to the glory of the Lord and let Him transform you into His image which will take you from His glory to glory not from defeat to despair.

§ Clean hands/pure heart principle.

§ Psalm 51:10 *"Create in me a clean heart, O God, And renew a steadfast spirit within me."*

§ Job 22:30 *"He will even deliver the one [for whom you intercede] who is not innocent; yes, he will be delivered through the cleanness of your hands.'* AMPC

Why do most of us never see 'from glory to glory'? Because we never let out all of the lies the enemy has trapped us with. We never stand in total surrender because we still want to control our circumstances, the people around us, and the direction of our lives.

§
Get rid of the lies and falsity, or hypocrisy, in yourself

I had to get so sick of me and what I wanted that I just laid it all down and allowed God to clean out what was displeasing to Him. Wouldn't you like to go from glory to glory? Be an outshining of His glory? I don't mean earthly success, but actual glory to glory. Then lay down your religious parameters of who God is and allow Him to clean out all that is not of Him. Maybe for the first time in your life you will really surrender to Him and His desire for you.

Psalm 26:8

*"LORD, I have loved the habitation of Your house,
And the place where Your glory dwells."*

David loved to be in the house of God because he could sense the glory of God. In Psalm 91 we see that there is no better place to be than in His presence, basking in His glory, filled with worship.

Psalm 91:1-7

*" He who dwells in the secret place of the Most High
shall abide under the shadow of the Almighty.
I will say of the LORD, "He is my refuge and my fortress;
my God, in Him I will trust."*

*Surely He shall deliver you from the snare of the fowler
and from the perilous pestilence.
He shall cover you with His feathers,
and under His wings you shall take refuge;
His truth shall be your shield and buckler.
You shall not be afraid of the terror by night,
nor of the arrow that flies by day,
nor of the pestilence that walks in darkness,
nor of the destruction that lays waste at noonday.*

*A thousand may fall at your side,
and ten thousand at your right hand;
but it shall not come near you."*

When we dwell in God's presence, in His secret place, He hears us. When we abide in Him, He is our refuge, our place of safety. He is also our fortress which keeps us safe from the enemy. He delivers us from

the attacks and assaults of the devil and not only that, the truth of God wraps around us like a shield and destroys the works of the enemy.

Please get a revelation that we were created to worship God and as we worship Him, He answers our prayers. He goes before us, with us and follows behind us, loving and caring for us as well as giving us the desires of our hearts. Get intimate with God because that is where the power to change resides.

Worship changes you totally and completely so that you can really say, *"it is no longer I who live, but Christ lives in me;"* (Galatians 2:20)

Prayer - Please Father, I come to You humbly. Teach me how to worship You. Show me how to enter into Your presence in that holy place where I will find grace and mercy to help in time of need, in Jesus' name, Amen.

> §
> Please get a revelation that we were created to worship God and stay in His presence.
>
> §
> Galatians 2:20 *"I have been crucified with Christ; it is no longer I who live, but Christ lives in me; and the life which I now live in the flesh I live by faith in the Son of God, who loved me and gave Himself for me."*

1. What gives us the right to go into the throne room of God? Use scriptures not in this lesson.

2. Are you a worshiper?

3. What is God telling you to do to change? What adjustments do you sense that He wants you to make?

4. Does God hear and answer your prayers? Use scripture.

"Here Am I"

Exodus 3:2-4 *"And the angel of the LORD appeared unto him in a flame of fire out of the midst of a bush: and he looked, and, behold, the bush burned with fire, and the bush was not consumed. And Moses said, I will now turn aside, and see this great sight, why the bush is not burnt. And when the LORD saw that he turned aside to see, God called unto him out of the midst of the bush, and said, 'Moses, Moses'. And he said, 'Here am I.'"* KJV

God appears to all of us many times throughout our lives; maybe not in a burning bush, but somehow and someway He manifests Himself to us. We have the choice to turn aside or to keep on going our own way. Moses stopped what he was doing. He allowed God to interrupt his life and change the course of his life as well as the lives of the children of Israel. Moses made a conscious decision to turn aside and hear God.

§ *Don't reason away God's voice.*

Many times, we hear God but instead of turning aside to hear what He has to say, we begin to rationalize or presume what He wants to tell us. God is touching all of us but not all of us turn aside and **see.** We can see with our natural eyes but a turning aside must be with our spiritual eyes as well.

There was a very definite time in my life where a bush was burning and I can see now that God was waiting for me to turn aside and **see,** because what came next changed my life, my family and innumerable others for the glory of God. Until I stopped my agenda, my ideas, my plans and turned aside to stand in the presence of an all-consuming God, I saw very little victory or power.

§ *Submit yourself to God.*

The next step of God speaking to us with His plan will not happen until we **stop**, turn aside, and look. God did not commission Moses until He saw that Moses had an obedient heart. Being a visionary does not make you fit for a vision of supernatural proportions but being obedient does. Moses got a vision when he turned aside with an obedient heart. That was when Moses heard the voice of the Lord and then he answered and said, "Here am I." Moses had to sense God, turn aside and open his heart to the voice of God so that he could then surrender his life for God's purpose and plan. Hallelujah!

God did not follow Moses around with a burning bush. Moses surrendered completely so that God's voice became familiar and His presence became a requirement in Moses' life.

Exodus 19:2-6 "*...So Israel camped there before the mountain. And Moses went up to God, and the LORD called to him from the mountain, saying, "Thus you shall say to the house of Jacob, and tell the children of Israel: 'You have seen what I did to the Egyptians, and how I bore you on eagles' wings and brought you to Myself. Now therefore, if you will indeed obey My voice and keep My covenant, then you shall be a special treasure to Me above all people; for all the earth is Mine. And you shall be to Me a kingdom of priests and a holy nation.'"*

§
Go up to the mountain of God.

The Word does not say that God descended on Moses but that Moses went up. Many times, obedience is an action. God called Moses to come up the mountain. Has He called you to come up a mountain of obedience? Is there an action that God is requiring of you that you haven't done yet? So many Christians proclaim they just want to be in the presence of God, yet do not stop, turn aside, listen, come up and separate themselves. Moses separated himself. He wanted to stay in God's presence but the people he led became afraid.

Exodus 20:18-20 "*Now all the people witnessed the thunderings, the lightning flashes, the sound of the trumpet, and the mountain smoking; and when the people saw it, they trembled and stood afar off. Then they said to Moses, "You speak with us, and we will hear; but let not God speak with us, lest we die." And Moses said to the people, "Do not fear; for God has come to test you, and that His fear may be before you, so that you may not sin."*"

Thunder can be felt, lightning seen, a trumpet heard, and smoke tasted. The people of Israel were enveloped with the presence of God and they allowed fear to keep them from **experiencing** God. They would rather have a man tell them what God said instead of God Himself. Many of us have been trapped in what our pastor says, the elders say, or whoever else is in authority, because we allow the devil to trap us with fear. This keeps us from stepping out and up into a spiritual realm that will touch every part of us.

Being a worshiper of God is not for the lazy who want to live off someone else's experience. It's for the ones who determine in their hearts to surrender completely to God and allow Him to direct their steps. I want to feel the thunder of God's presence and see the lightening of the miracles cascading across the earth by the power of the Holy Spirit. I want to hear the trumpet of God's voice and taste His Word as it goes forth from my mouth.

The next verse is heartbreaking to me because I have seen this over and over from God's people: *"So the people stood afar off, but Moses drew near the thick darkness where God was."* (Exodus 20:21)

The people stood afar off. "Oh God, do not let us be a people that stand afar off. Let us be a people that draw near to You, to that place of power and glory. I want to feel Your love and hear Your voice. Your Word says that I will follow the voice of the Shepherd and not follow the voice of another. I desire to see Your works and taste and see that You are good. Oh God immerse me in Your Spirit and give me a heart to turn aside, to see, come up and walk in the presence of a living God, in Jesus' name."

§
Joshua stayed behind in the presence of God.

Exodus 33:7-11 *"Moses always erected the sacred tent (the "Tent for Meeting with God," he called it) far outside the camp, and everyone who wanted to consult with Jehovah went out there. Whenever Moses went to the Tabernacle, all the people, when they saw it, stood and would rise and stand in their tent doors. As he entered, the pillar of cloud would come down and stand at the door while the Lord spoke with Moses. Then all the people worshiped from their tent doors, bowing low to the pillar of cloud. Inside the tent the Lord spoke to Moses face to face, as a man speaks to his friend. Afterwards Moses would return to the camp, but the young man who assisted him, Joshua (son of Nun), stayed behind in the Tabernacle."* TLB

The Lord spoke to Moses face to face. God knew Moses as a friend. Moses went out to meet God and the people were content to stand at the doorways of their tents and worship God, all but one young man who was following hard after God and God's man.

Many Christians, good people, really don't desire to seek God's face because there is a lot of personal life adjustments that will have to be made. You can't seek God's face with a life full of sin. You may love God dearly, you may even desire to be different but until you deal with whatever is displeasing to God, you will not be a face seeker. Most people seek God for His answers to their prayers, and He does answer our prayers. If you are satisfied with that then this Bible study will either make you angry or hungry for more of God. I was a satisfied believer for many years and then I became hungry for God and the things of God. When you stand face to face with God as Moses did then you can ask to see His glory.

Joshua would stay behind in the Tabernacle after Moses was done speaking to God. Joshua would stay in the presence and in the place of visitation. The Lord would come down in a pillar of cloud, the glory

cloud, and Joshua would stay in that atmosphere, that place of visitation even after Moses was gone. Joshua saw God and he saw God's man and he stayed in a place of submission not only to God but also to God's man, Moses. He stayed in that place of miracles and he was rewarded for that faithfulness.

Numbers 27:15-23, "*Then Moses spoke to the LORD, saying: "Let the LORD, the God of the spirits of all flesh, set a man over the congregation, who may go out before them and go in before them, who may lead them out and bring them in, that the congregation of the LORD may not be like sheep which have no shepherd." And the LORD said to Moses: "Take Joshua the son of Nun with you, a man in whom is the Spirit, and lay your hand on him; set him before Eleazar the priest and before all the congregation, and inaugurate him in their sight. And you shall give some of your authority to him, that all the congregation of the children of Israel may be obedient. He shall stand before Eleazar the priest, who shall inquire before the LORD for him by the judgment of the Urim; at his word they shall go out, and at his word they shall come in, he and all the children of Israel with him--all the congregation." So Moses did as the LORD commanded him. He took Joshua and set him before Eleazar the priest and before all the congregation. And he laid his hands on him and inaugurated him, just as the LORD commanded by the hand of Moses."*

God told Moses to lay hands on Joshua, *"a man in whom is the Spirit,"* and pass the authority or the mantel on to him. What God ordered Moses to do in the physical realm God did in the spiritual realm. The mantel of God's anointing passed on to Joshua because Joshua chose to stay in God's presence.

> § The mantel of God's anointing passed on to Joshua because Joshua chose to stay in God's presence.

Prayer - Father, make us a man or woman in whom Your Spirit dwells where we can stay in Your presence. Dear Lord, I want to see You face to face and be known as a friend of God. Let me recognize my season of visitation and commission, in Jesus' name, Amen.

1. What did Moses do when he saw the burning bush? Have you had a symbolic burning bush in your life? What did you do?

2. Do you have a desire to sense God and turn aside from your busy life to get a commission from Him? Do you desire to spend time with Him, to rest in His presence as Joshua did?

3. What steps do you sense God wants you to take spiritually to align yourself with Him?

4. What do you sense God wants to do with you, for you and through you?

"You will not need to fight in this battle. Position yourselves, stand still and see the salvation of the LORD"

2 Chronicles 17:3-6, *"Now the LORD was with Jehoshaphat, because he walked in the former ways of his father David; he did not seek the Baals, but sought the God of his father, and walked in His commandments and not according to the acts of Israel. Therefore the LORD established the kingdom in his hand; and all Judah gave presents to Jehoshaphat, and he had riches and honor in abundance. And his heart took delight in the ways of the LORD; moreover he removed the high places and wooden images from Judah."*

These verses explain what God will do for a person who will worship Him and walk in His ways. The Lord established Jehoshaphat's kingdom, putting it in a firm place. God secured Jehoshaphat's kingdom, making it stable. Jehoshaphat had *"riches and honor in abundance."* Not only did God make the kingdom secure but the Lord blessed Jehoshaphat through the people. *"For it is God who gives us the ability to get wealth."* (Deuteronomy 8:18) It was Jehoshaphat's job to love, worship, and obey God and it was God's job to prosper his way.

Jehoshaphat was honored and made wealthy but he was also a man of integrity. He not only took delight in the ways of the Lord, he tore down the high places. Those are the places of worship of false gods. Removing the high places is taking down all of the false gods and idols that had been allowed to enter into the hearts of God's people. They were the false gods of the area or the people they had conquered and they didn't destroy them when God gave them the victory over all of their enemies. They learned to live with them and soon they couldn't live without them. These high places are addressed several times in the Old Testament. There were many who didn't tear down the high places and these scriptures explain to you God's decision because of their disobedience. Leviticus 26:30, Numbers 33:52-56, Deuteronomy 12:2-4 and there are many other references besides these in the Old Testament. Integrity will take you where riches cannot keep you and He rewards faithfulness. God honored and blessed Jehoshaphat because he *"took delight in the ways of the Lord."* There comes a day when you must believe God and step out in obedience.

2 Chronicles 20:1-4 *"It happened after this that the people of Moab with the people of Ammon, and others with them besides the Ammonites, came to battle against Jehoshaphat. Then some came*

§
There comes a day when you must believe God and step out in obedience.

and told Jehoshaphat, saying, 'A great multitude is coming against you from beyond the sea, from Syria; and they are in Hazazon Tamar' (which is En Gedi). And Jehoshaphat feared, and set himself to seek the LORD, and proclaimed a fast throughout all Judah. So Judah gathered together to ask help from the LORD; and from all the cities of Judah they came to seek the LORD."

> §
> Believe what God tells you.
>
> Listen to His instructions and do them.
>
> Praise Him even in the midst of battle.
>
> Watch God keep His promise to you.

Jehoshaphat had a problem that honor and riches couldn't solve. A great multitude was coming against the Israelites and they needed God. Many of us feel like we are in the midst of a war but how often do we turn to our own answers or the answers of those around us? Jehoshaphat was a worshiper and a warrior and he sought for an answer from God. We will all go through temptations and attacks of the enemy, but our faith is in God. We must get to the place that we seek Him in everything first instead of last after we've tried everything else.

Jehoshaphat was surrounded by the enemy and in the natural world it looked like disaster. But he understood that he served a God Who moved in the supernatural to fight this battle for him. Sometimes we must fight the enemy in prayer and understanding and then there are times when we just start praising God and He defeats the enemy for us. Do you know which kind of battle you are in now? Is it the kind that you need to take authority over the enemy and command him away from your family and circumstances? Or is it the kind that God says, "I've already won this battle just praise me."? He already has both instances covered but He wants us to seek Him and actually hear what He tells us to do. That is what happened in these next verses. They got their orders from God, not reasoning. Reason will tell you to do it the same way you did last time when you experienced victory. The voice of God will tell you what is required at **this** time to defeat the enemy.

2 Chronicles 20:14-18, *"Then the Spirit of the LORD came upon Jahaziel the son of Zechariah, the son of Benaiah, the son of Jeiel, the son of Mattaniah, a Levite of the sons of Asaph, in the midst of the assembly. And he said, "Listen, all you of Judah and you inhabitants of Jerusalem, and you, King Jehoshaphat! Thus says the LORD to you: 'Do not be afraid nor dismayed because of this great multitude, for the battle is not yours, but God's. Tomorrow go down against them. They will surely come up by the Ascent of Ziz, and you will find them at the end of the brook before the Wilderness of Jeruel. You will not need to fight in this battle. Position yourselves, stand still and see the salvation of the LORD, who is with you, O Judah and Jerusalem!' Do not fear or be dismayed; tomorrow go out against them, for the LORD*

is with you." And Jehoshaphat bowed his head with his face to the ground, and all Judah and the inhabitants of Jerusalem bowed before the LORD, worshiping the LORD."

The Spirit of the Lord spoke through a prophet and told Jehoshaphat not to be afraid because the battle was God's. It can be so hard for us to understand that God will really fight our battles. All we have to do is listen and do as He says and not get in the way.

The Lord told them where the enemy would be and then He said to *"position yourselves and stand still."* God gave them a place and a plan and all they had to do was be in the right place at the right time. The Lord said not to fear because He would be there and He would be their salvation.

Jehoshaphat believed God and he and his people bowed their heads in worship. They worshiped God and the next morning they got up early. They did not drag their feet complaining all the way. They got up early and Jehoshaphat put the singers in front and as they *"began to sing and praise, the Lord set ambushes against the people of Ammon, Moab, and Mount Seir, who had come against Judah; and they were defeated."* As we praise God, God goes to war. Jehoshaphat had a love relationship with God and he was a worshiper first before he was a warrior. The next two verses explain that the enemies slaughtered each other and when Jehoshaphat and his people got to the place God told them to go to, the enemy was already dead.

Jehoshaphat had a word from God and he had a heart to please God. Sometimes we get a word from God but fear gets in the middle and we do not do exactly what God tells us to do. Do not let fear trap you in defeat, the battle is not ours but God's. In this case Jehoshaphat was told not to war but to sing and praise. In some cases, they were told to war and the enemy would be given into their hands. Do not try to figure God out, just believe Him, worship Him and trust that He is God and He will prosper your way.

Prayer - Father, I ask that You give me such a heart of worship that when You say stop, I'll stop. When You say go, I'll go. I want to worship You in the 'beauty of Your holiness.' I desire to understand the battle is always Yours whether it is won by worship or warfare. Give me a heart to know Your ways, in Jesus' name I pray.

§
Do not let fear trap you in defeat!

1. Why did God honor Jehoshaphat?

2. What were God's instructions?

3. Find another example of warfare in scripture.

4. Could you have followed God's instructions? If no, then what must you do to align yourself with God in obedience and worship?

HEARING GOD IS NOT A PROGRAM BUT A LIFESTYLE

2 Samuel 5:10, 17 "*So David went on and became great, and the LORD God of hosts was with him. 17 Now when the Philistines heard that they had anointed David king over Israel, all the Philistines went up to search for David. And David heard of it and went down to the stronghold.*"

God was with David. The scriptures tell us that Saul had become afraid of David because God was with him and that God had departed from Saul. When you begin to walk in God's presence even people who know the Lord will become afraid and, in some cases, even angry.

Walking in God's will for your life will not necessarily make you popular with the religious establishment or those in authority either. But there comes a time when God shows to the world whom He has chosen or anointed. David became great because he loved to worship God. He learned to worship with his harp and his voice and he learned to war with his hands and his spirit. He listened to the inner voice of the Holy Spirit and he learned to obey.

When the prophet Samuel rebuked King Saul for his disobedience to the commandments of God in 1 Samuel 13:14, he told the king that God was looking for a man after His own heart. Later in 1 Samuel 16:13, Samuel anointed David king *"and the Spirit of the Lord came upon him from that day forward."*

In the opening verses of the 5th chapter of 2 Samuel, the Word states that the Philistines heard that David was anointed king and they went to search for him. The world will always hunt down those anointed by God. David heard that he was being hunted and he went to a safe place where he could inquire from God what he was to do. Many times when we come under attack from the enemy, we need to separate ourselves and get to a safe place and wait on a Word from God. We need to forget our reasoning because too many times the devil will talk us out of a victory designed by God. This is where you need that close intimacy with God so that you know the difference between God's voice and the voice of the great deceiver and the father of lies.

2 Samuel 5:19-25, "*So David inquired of the LORD, saying, "Shall I go up against the Philistines? Will You deliver them into my hand?" And the LORD said to David, "Go up, for I will doubtless deliver the Philistines into your hand." So David went to Baal Perazim, and David defeated them there; and he said, "The LORD has broken*

> § David listened to the inner voice of the Holy Spirit and he learned to obey.

through my enemies before me, like a breakthrough of water." Therefore he called the name of that place Baal Perazim. And they left their images there, and David and his men carried them away. Then the Philistines went up once again and deployed themselves in the Valley of Rephaim. Therefore David inquired of the LORD, He said, "You shall not go up; circle around behind them, and come upon them in front of the mulberry trees. And it shall be, when you hear the sound of marching in the tops of the mulberry trees, then you shall advance quickly. For then the LORD will go out before you to strike the camp of the Philistines." And David did so, as the LORD commanded him; and he drove back the Philistines from Geba as far as Gezer."

§ The Lord of the breakthrough.

In verse nineteen the Lord tells David that He will deliver the enemy into his hands. The Lord did what He said He would do and David called God a God of breakthroughs. Many of you are looking for a breakthrough. In order to have a breakthrough something must be broken through and that requires war. Just as a violent movement of water can break through a levy or dam, God broke through the enemy and David gave the credit to God and named the place *"the Lord breaks through"*.

The enemy did not stop. They came at David again. The enemy does the same thing to us. Far too many times we receive a breakthrough and we believe that the enemy will just give up. Many dreams and visions are abandoned because we are not aware there can be another attack and we get discouraged and give up instead of going back into battle again.

David inquired again and God gave him different instructions. Do not take your last instructions from God and use them for the next war. God gives us new plans and strategies to win the battles; otherwise we depend on ourselves and what we know instead of Him and His omnipotence.

The Lord said specifically that this strategy was different and not to go up against them but instead to circle around behind them and wait. The circling around is the easy part. It is the waiting that is the tough part. We love for God to give us something tangible to do. It is the next part where many of us miss it.

David was to wait and listen. Listening is not passive. Listening is a quietness of the spirit so that you can hear and feel the movement in the heavenly realm. David was to listen for the *"sound of marching in the tops of the mulberry trees"*. This was the sound of the angelic

armies of God going before David and his army to strike the camp of the Philistines.

So many of us have become dull of hearing when it comes to listening to God because He takes longer to speak to us than a thirty second commercial. Listening takes practice and diligence. Sometimes we may not get it right, but praise God, He will fix our mistakes. He knows our hearts and He loves us. If we miss the mark all we have to do is ask for forgiveness, receive His forgiveness and go again. Failing is not being a failure, it is being human. God knows my heart and that I have surrendered it to Him but sometimes I make a mistake. So what! It is not on purpose and He knows that and He loves me. Ask the Lord to open your spiritual ears so that you can hear Him when He gives you the plans, purposes and battle strategies for your life.

§
Waiting can be hard.

God gave David different instructions and David listened. Many of us would go ahead and do what we know to do instead of going back to God and getting new orders. New orders mean God is running the show and not us. Hallelujah!

First, David asked God what to do. Then he obeyed and it worked. The same problem came back around and this is where many of us miss it. We go with the last thing God told us to do when the reality is He wants to do something different. David did not fall into that trap. He inquired again. He was given different instructions. David was told to move in behind the enemy and then to wait because God was sending armies of angels. It is the waiting that is the difficult part because we must believe that we heard God and that He will do what He said He would.

Moses, David and Jehoshaphat sought God. Moses turned aside from his daily schedule and encountered God through a miracle. He had been trained all his life to fulfill God's destiny for him. David was a boy when he knew that he had been chosen by God to be the king over God's children. David learned early that his life was not his own but that God's call on him superseded whatever plans he might have had. Jehoshaphat was already a king when he encountered God in a real and tangible way. *"His heart took delight in the ways of the Lord."* (2 Chronicles 17:5). The verse does not say that Jehoshaphat took delight in his riches and honor which God gave him in abundance. The Word says that *"his heart took delight in the ways of the Lord."* In these three examples, God delivered through miracles, worship and warfare. Moses saw God face to face. David was a man after God's

own heart. The Lord was with Jehoshaphat because he walked in the ways of his father David. who loved and worshiped God.

We are not warring against people. *"We do not wrestle against flesh and blood, but against principalities, against powers, against the rulers of the darkness of this age, against spiritual hosts of wickedness in the heavenly places."* (Ephesians 6:12)

This book is to teach you worship and warfare. Hearing God is not a program but a lifestyle. Some of you may never have quieted down enough to hear anything. Some of you may believe that God does not talk to us anymore. Both of those are wrong. God is the same yesterday, today and forever. If He talked before then He talks now. We are not here to tell God what we want to do for Him we are to let God tell us His plans and His purposes for our life.

Prayer - Father make me a man/woman after Your own heart. Give me eyes that behold the beauty of Your holiness and ears that hear You when You whisper my name. Let me dwell where Your glory dwells and let me abide in Your presence, in Jesus' name.

§
The battle is against the Enemy.
Listen to God, believe what He says and go forth in victory.

1. What was the first thing that David did when he heard the Philistines were coming against him? Use Scripture reference.

2. What was the strategy that God gave David? There were seven steps to this victory.

3. What strategy has God given you for ministry?

4. Where have you missed God and what do you need to change?

Chapter 4

"Do not fear, for those who are with us are more than those who are with them."

Ephesians 6:11-12 "*Put on all of God's armor so that you will be able to stand safe against all strategies and tricks of Satan. For we are not fighting against people made of flesh and blood, but against persons without bodies-the evil rulers of the unseen world, those mighty satanic beings and great evil princes of darkness who rule this world; and against huge numbers of wicked spirits in the spirit world.*" TLB

People are not the enemy although the devil uses people. If you can fully understand this, you will endure until the end with victory and with the joy of the Lord. We have all been hurt by well-meaning Christians and because of that many of us never make it to the next level. We stay trapped by hurt and disappointment in a place of very little joy and almost no victory.

We have such a short time to be on this earth. God has not left us here to point out everyone's faults or to condemn the world or to walk away from those in need. Get a revelation. If the devil cannot take you to hell, then he will try to neutralize you and the affects you have on others so that you are of no good to yourself or those around you. You will become a POW. You belong to God but you can be imprisoned by a critical spirit, condemning attitude, hurt, anger and possibly fear. Too often we put the face of harsh and critical humans on the face of God.

God's love is so great that He sent His Son to die for us carrying our sin so that we could be free to worship Him, live for Him and when the time comes, to die and resurrect with Him. So lay down all of that unforgiveness, hurt, anger, fear or whatever it is, and command it to die in Jesus' name. Then, pick up unconditional love, joy, hope, healing, and faith, and allow God to train you as a soldier of the cross.

God is a God of mercy and compassion as well as judgment. Determine in your heart to love unconditionally. Love is unconditional, trust is earned. Jesus loved unconditionally but He did not trust everyone. He said that men's hearts were evil yet He came that all men might live.

We are fighting against *"evil rulers of the unseen world, mighty satanic beings, great evil princes and a huge number of wicked*

§ We are fighting evil rulers of the unseen world.

§ Ask to see the battle from God's perspective from heaven down and quit looking at it from earth up.

spirits." There is no way that we can be victorious if we do not accept this knowledge and act on it. These beings cannot be defeated by our humanness but only by the power of the Holy Spirit.

I once attended a women's conference and the woman heading up the conference was an ex-high priestess in voodoo. When she began to speak, I felt in my spirit that something was wrong. As the evening progressed, I saw that she was casting spells on the unsuspecting women. She explained that she was going to take us to heaven to stand in the presence of God. We were all going to go together and He would reveal mysteries to us. She went on and explained that Paul was enlightened when the scales came on his eyes on the road to Damascus. That is an untrue statement. Paul was blinded when the scales came on his eyes. She had all of the women asking God to put scales on their eyes so that they could be enlightened. All those who asked entered into the deception. The next day we were told to stretch our spirits and join her on this trip to heaven. This type of practice is eastern mysticism and I watched as over one hundred women knelt and joined their spirit to hers for the journey. I was angry. I was horrified remembering that unless Jesus came back early even the very elect would be deceived. (Matthew 24:24) My friends and I left at that time. I heard later from a woman who stayed the whole time that the next day they all joined their spirits with this woman to go to hell to save a fractured soul.

> §
> Ask for God to give you the ability to recognize a lie because the Truth, which is His Word, is so much a part of you.

They had lost the battle when they did not recognize an untruth and went into deception. These women lifting their hands for the scales to be placed on their eyes were not evil. They were ignorant of the enemy, ignorant of the scriptures and seeking an experience instead of the Creator of experiences. I love experiences. Salvation is an experience but you must have the Word in you to be more than a conqueror. Was this woman my enemy? No, but she was and is in error at the very least. I pray that she comes to the saving knowledge of Jesus Christ and I leave her to God. I alerted those that I am serving in ministry to beware and never join their spirit with anyone else's. Our spirit is to be filled with the Holy Spirit and at His command. The days are growing evil. Please ask for God to give you the ability to recognize a lie because the Truth, which is His Word, is so much a part of you.

In 2 Kings 6:8-12, the king of Syria was warring against Israel. Elisha would send word to the king of Israel about the king of Syria's plans and movements. Elisha knew the plans of the enemy because God revealed them to him in prayer.

Amos 3:7 *"Surely the Lord GOD does nothing, unless He reveals His secret to His servants the prophets."*

Are you sensitive to the Holy Spirit? Does He reveal secrets to you? Pray for sensitivity of your spirit to His Spirit and study the Word so that you can divide the lie from the truth. God took me to that conference so that I could see a deception and I thank Him that His Word has become such a part of me that even if I had not known deliverance, I would have recognized an untruth.

When the king of Syria learned that the problem was Elisha, he came against him.

2 Kings 6:13-18 *"So he said, "Go and see where he is, that I may send and get him." And it was told him, saying, "Surely he is in Dothan." Therefore he sent horses and chariots and a great army there, and they came by night and surrounded the city. And when the servant of the man of God arose early and went out, there was an army, surrounding the city with horses and chariots. And his servant said to him, "Alas, my master! What shall we do?" So he answered, "Do not fear, for those who are with us are more than those who are with them." And Elisha prayed, and said, "LORD, I pray, open his eyes that he may see." Then the LORD opened the eyes of the young man, and he saw. And behold, the mountain was full of horses and chariots of fire all around Elisha. So when the Syrians came down to him, Elisha prayed to the LORD, and said, "Strike this people, I pray, with blindness." And He struck them with blindness according to the word of Elisha."*

§
Every miracle in the Bible started as a problem.

The enemy will come at night and surround you and the place you are in. He will come with huge opposition threatening you, your mission, and your life. This is where you have to see the enemy. The servant of God arises early because of what comes next. Elisha's servant did not need to awaken Elisha. Elisha already had sensed God's presence and the presence of the army of the Lord. Elisha prayed that his servant would see God's might which was surrounding God's man. Not only did God send His warring angels to surround Elisha, but He also brought down the enemy with blindness. The enemy was led away by God and His man and then kindness took all the fight out of them.

Elisha knew that he was not fighting against flesh and blood. We need to get that revelation. Seek to be sensitive to the Holy Spirit, desire to be a kingdom walker, a visionary, and a vessel of honor. *"Put on all of God's armor so that you will be able to **stand safe** against all strategies and tricks of Satan."* [emphasis added]

Prayer - Oh, Father fill me with Your Spirit and let me sense Your presence. Let me see with spiritual eyes and hear with spiritual ears. Give me a heart to seek You and the eyes of a warrior. Show me the war and let me always show forth the light of Christ. In the name of Jesus and by His blood I am more than a conqueror.

1. Do you have eyes that see, not just physical eyes, but spiritual eyes to see?

2. Who was afraid when they saw the enemy and who was not afraid? Do you battle fear? What must you do to conquer it?

3. Are you a servant of man or a servant of God?

4. What is God telling you to do to change and line yourself up with Him?

ASK TO DIE TO SELF

Joshua 3:5 *"And Joshua said to the people, "Sanctify yourselves, for tomorrow the LORD will do wonders among you."*

The people were told to sanctify themselves, or set themselves apart from anything unclean, and to devote themselves to God and the things of God. Victory comes with time spent in the presence of the living God. You cannot be an effective warrior for God without being a priest first. The next verses in Joshua describe trust and faith in a living God. The people were told to select twelve men to lead the tribes and that the ark which held the Word of God would cross the Jordan first.

The priests who carried the ark with the Word would step into the river first and the water would be cut off. Are you a worshiper and do you carry the Word of God inside yourself? If so, God is saying put your feet to the path that He has directed for you to go and believe Him. The people believed God and those who knew God carried His Word and stepped out into His plan. As soon as their feet touched the water God did what He said He would. He made the water to stand up in a heap upstream. I love the next verse:

Joshua 3:17 *"Then the priests who bore the ark of the covenant of the LORD stood firm on dry ground in the midst of the Jordan; and all Israel crossed over on dry ground, until all the people had crossed completely over the Jordan."*

The priests who knew the Word and carried the Word, stood firm. The earth was not unstable but firm and dry. God will not send you into quicksand but onto dry, firm ground when you know and obey His Word. The ground will be stable and you will be as well. We are to be leaders or priests to an unsaved world offering to them the Word of God, safety, and a good witness so that we can say as Paul did, *"follow me as I follow Christ."* (1 Corinthians 11:1)

God did not just save the priests who carried His Word. He saved all those who would cross over. God also instructed them to build a memorial of stones where the feet of the priests had stood. We need to understand from where God has brought us, what He has done for us, and how He has answered our prayers. We need to build a history with Him. If you do not journal you should. Journaling will help you keep a better record of His answering your prayers and you will see more clearly what has transpired as you walk this life out with God. God is

§
Sanctify yourselves.

§
The Lord will do wonders.

not a random God but a God of order. Victories do not just happen, they are built and they start when you determine to set yourself apart or sanctify yourself unto God and the things of God.

2 Corinthians 4:8-9 "*We are hard pressed on every side, yet not crushed; we are perplexed, but not in despair; persecuted, but not forsaken; struck down, but not destroyed—*"

We all go through things but it is how we come out on the other side that counts. We are not crushed, in despair, forsaken, nor destroyed. Take heart we are being set apart and dying to our flesh. Dying to flesh is painful but mandatory to be surrendered and obedient unto God. As long as you and your flesh are number one in your life then you are on the throne and Jesus is not. Ask for forgiveness, get down and die. We all have to do this if we are going to affect a lost and dying world. I still remember how painful dying was as I realized that I had no right to anything of me. My personality, if it didn't please God, needed to be changed by Him. My sense of humor wasn't governed by the wisdom of God, so I needed it to die, a sometimes painful death, as I asked forgiveness from people that I just shared an off color joke with. God wants to use us in magnificent and powerful ways but He won't use a fool. Be cautious with what you think is funny. It may in reality be foolish.

2 Corinthians 4:10-12 "*always carrying about in the body the dying of the Lord Jesus, that the life of Jesus also may be manifested in our body. For we who live are always delivered to death for Jesus' sake, that the life of Jesus also may be manifested in our mortal flesh. So then death is working in us, but life in you.*"

In order to be changed into the image of Christ we must ask to die. A famous author states in one of his books that those who ask to die, die quicker. That is a heart of obedience and tenderness towards God. If we die to ourselves then the compassion of Christ will pour from our eyes, the Word of God will spill from our mouths, and our hearts will be undivided and our hands will do the works of Jesus. Jesus said *"greater things will you do than I have done because I go to be with my Father"*. (John 14:12) If we die then God will use us to bring life to others because the life of Christ will show forth from us.

2 Corinthians 4:13 "*And since we have the same spirit of faith, according to what is written,* **"I believed and therefore I spoke,"** *we also believe and therefore speak,*" [emphasis added]

§
We all have trials and tribulations.

§
John 16:33 *"These things I have spoken to you, that in Me you may have peace. In the world you will have tribulation; but be of good cheer, I have overcome the world."*

§
In order to be changed into the image of Jesus we must ask to die.

Since we have the same spirit or attitude of faith then we can speak out boldly, "I believe, therefore I speak." I want that same attitude, that attitude of sanctification, of death, of life, and of faith. I believe God's Word and I am determined to share the gospel boldly, *"heal the brokenhearted, to proclaim liberty to the captives and the opening of the prison to those who are bound."* (Luke 4:18)

Prayer - Give me a heart that believes and a mouth that speaks Your Words with compassion and power so that I will make a difference everywhere You send me, in Jesus' name I pray, Amen.

1. What holds your heart and what are you determined to do?

2. Are you willing to step into the water of obedience?

3. What is God telling you to do in order to sanctify yourself? Use scripture.

4. What do you believe?

SURRENDER AND OBEY!

Psalm 143:8-10

*"Cause me to hear Your lovingkindness in the morning,
For in You do I trust;
cause me to know the way in which I should walk,
for I lift up my soul to You.*

*Deliver me, O LORD, from my enemies;
in You I take shelter.
Teach me to do Your will,
for You are my God;
Your Spirit is good.
Lead me in the land of uprightness."*

§ Did you get up expecting to hear God's voice?

Do you get up in the morning expecting to hear God's lovingkindness? That means God speaks to us and we are to hear it. This scripture states that if we listen to God because we trust Him, He will let us know what we are to do. He will protect us from our enemies. He will shelter us, He will teach us, and He will lead us to do good and honorable things.

Unfortunately, this is where many of us hear the voice of the devil expounding on our past and this is where you must get radical. We all have a past, Paul had a past. He was a killer of Christians. But he had to let go of Saul of Tarsus the persecutor of Christians so that he could become Paul the apostle who would write much of the New Testament.

Philippians 3:13-14 *"...but one thing I do, forgetting those things which are behind and reaching forward to those things which are ahead, I press toward the goal for the prize of the upward call of God in Christ Jesus."*

§ Rebuke the devil!

Rebuke the devil! If you are submitted to God then Satan must flee from you. Paul let his past go. He was submitted to God and that upward call of God in Christ Jesus. Paul was submitted and obedient unto God and He spoke to him by His Holy Spirit.

Acts 16:6-10 *"Now when they had gone through Phrygia and the region of Galatia, they were forbidden by the Holy Spirit to preach the Word in Asia. After they had come to Mysia, they tried to go into Bithynia, but the Spirit did not permit them. So passing by Mysia, they came down to Troas. And a vision appeared to Paul in the night. A man of Macedonia stood and pleaded with him, saying, "Come over*

to Macedonia and help us." Now after he had seen the vision, immediately we sought to go to Macedonia, concluding that the Lord had called us to preach the gospel to them."

What happened here? Paul listened to the Holy Spirit's direction not once but twice and then God gave him a vision in the night. Would he have received the vision if he had not obeyed the Holy Spirit? It is unlikely. He would have been in the wrong place at the wrong time. This is called being out of the perfect will of God. Would Paul still have been a Christian? Absolutely. Would God still love Paul? Absolutely. Would Paul have missed a huge opportunity? Absolutely.

Paul listened, was told what to do, and the Philippian church was birthed, which was the most faithful to support Paul as he finished his course. God spoke, gave a plan, and then led Paul to Lydia to start a church in Philippi. Paul did what God told him to do. He spread the gospel and even cast out a demon from a young girl. If you read the entire story you will see that he was also beaten and imprisoned. But there as he and Silas were praising God, the prison was shaken by a violent earthquake which led to the jailer and his entire household being saved. God did not say that there was not going to be persecution, but as we follow His plans and strategies, He will shake our enemies and force them to loose us. Praise God!

Are you praising Him even in the midst of prison? He is big enough to get you out, praise Him! Trust God. He will show you the way you should walk, deliver you from your enemies, teach you, and lead you into living an honorable life full of joy and power by His grace. God may speak to you through dreams, visions, His Word, by His Spirit, through other believers, and / or your circumstances. Get up and learn about Him.

2 Timothy 2:15 *"Study to shew thyself approved unto God, a workman that needeth not to be ashamed, rightly dividing the word of truth."* KJV

God will speak to you but your ability to listen is dependent on your level of surrender and obedience. God will speak to you and give you plans and purposes that are to be accomplished through you by the Holy Spirit. Surrender and obey!

§
Paul listened to the Holy Spirit and God gave him a vision for his next assignment.

§
Are you missing your God assignment because you listened to man?

§
God will speak to you but your ability to listen is dependent on your level of surrender and obedience.

Prayer - Father open my eyes so that I may see. Give me the strength to sanctify myself, set myself apart, and the wisdom to hear You, trust You, and know the way, because You will deliver me from my enemies. Teach me to do Your will so that I may walk in Your ways all the days of my life to bring glory and honor unto Jesus and Him alone. Amen.

1. How does God speak to us? Use scriptures for examples.

2. Do you listen as well as talk?

3. What must you do to change or to align yourself more with the Word of God?

4. What is a strategy that God is giving you?

CLEAN HANDS AND PURE HEART PRINCIPLE

Matthew 10:1 *"And when He had called unto Him His twelve disciples, He gave them power against unclean spirits, to cast them out, and to heal all manner of sickness and all manner of disease."* KJV

§ Why do we need clean hands?

We are to be disciples of Christ. He has given us the power to cast out demons and heal sickness and disease. We can be bound by demons including sickness and disease. Many times, the sickness or disease is demonic and when a demon is cast out, the person is healed. All sickness and disease comes from the devil because it came into the garden when Adam and Eve sinned.

A very famous preacher's wife had cancer of the bowel a few years ago. It was caused because her diet consisted mainly of sandwiches rather than fruits and vegetables. This is not demonic but instead poor food choices done in ignorance of the consequences. So we see that not all illness is demonic. However, I have worked with many abused women who suffered with fibromyalgia, asthma, or bronchitis because of their abuse and they received their healing after going through prayers of deliverance

Jesus' blood makes us righteous, or in right standing with God, but the Word also says in Psalm 66:18, *"If I regard iniquity in my heart, the Lord will not hear."* We are able to set the captives free by the power given to us through Jesus Christ and if we want God to hear and answer our prayers, we need to pray effectively with passion, and with a clear conscience.

When David was turning back to the Lord, repenting of his sin with Bathsheba, he wrote Psalm 51. In Psalm 51:10-11, He said, *"Create in me a clean heart, O God, and renew a steadfast spirit within me. Do not cast me away from Your presence, and do not take Your Holy Spirit from me."* We must allow God to create in us a clean heart so that we can be an effective, fervent, and righteous man or woman. We are to examine ourselves and allow God to cleanse all that is not of Him from us.

Psalm 24:3-4

*"Who may ascend into the hill of the LORD?
Or who may stand in His holy place?
He who has clean hands and a pure heart,
who has not lifted up his soul to an idol,
nor sworn deceitfully."*

The clean hands and pure heart principle is very necessary as explained by Job in chapter 22 verse 30: "*He will even deliver the one [for whom you intercede] who is not innocent; yes, he will be delivered through the cleanness of your hands.*" AMPC

God will set free, or save and deliver someone who is not innocent simply because of the cleanness of your hands. That is the clean hands and pure heart principle. The Lord may be speaking to you right now about something within you that you have never taken care of. Either ask for forgiveness or forgive someone else so that your heart is pure before God. Command any demons that may be there associated with that sin or that unforgiveness to leave you now in the name of Jesus.

> §
> We are to set the captives free. This is our job.

Please remember to deal with the demons that come with the sin. Many are teaching programs that deal with sin and unforgiveness but they do not tell you to command all demons associated with that sin or a person to leave in the name of Jesus. Demons can be transferred not just generationally but also from the person who abused you. So you need to ask God to sever all natural ties or unnatural ties [for family members or spouse] to that person. Then you command all demons associated with that person and that sin to leave you, body and soul in the name of Jesus. Then ask God to fill you with the Holy Spirit, with healing, love, holiness, purity or whatever is the godly opposite of what you just commanded out.

We are to set the captives free. This is our job. Jesus gave us that authority before He was crucified and then again just before He was received in heaven and sat down at the right hand of God. The keys of the kingdom are binding and loosing and we are to wield those keys. Do not ask God to bind away demons or to set your husband, wife or child free. That authority has already been passed to you. You are to bind and loose and you are to cast out demons in the name of Jesus if you are a believer. In Webster's Dictionary the word belief means to accept things as truth. How many of us Christians just want to make it into heaven and we have no desire, or we are ignorant about the power that is to work within us. Not everyone has been prepared to do this so if this is new to you and either you or someone you love needs deliverance you can contact me through the website.

Prayer- I thank You, Father, that the Bible states in John 14:12 that I will do greater works than Jesus has done because He has gone to You, ever interceding for me. I want to be that man or woman after Your own heart and believe. I trust that You will guide me through Your word and godly, trustworthy people that You place in my path, in Jesus' name I pray.

1. Are you operating in the clean hands and pure heart principle? If not, what do you have to deal with to get to that place?

2. Find other healing scriptures besides the ones in this chapter's lessons and write them down.

3. Do you know how to cast out a demon? Do this now for yourself if the Lord is giving you something that you need to take care of?

    a) Recognize the problem.

    b) Deal with the sin, unforgiveness, etc.

    c) Ask God to sever natural or unnatural ties to whomever.

    d) Command all demons associated with that sin or person to leave body and soul in Jesus' name. Ask God to pour out His Spirit with godly opposite of what you just commanded out such as hatred-love, unclean-holiness, etc.

Sample Prayer- I ask You Father to sever all unnatural ties that bind me to (name) in the spiritual and physical realms in Jesus' name. I forgive them for the abuse or sin that they did to me and I let them go. I ask Father that You cleanse me of that sin and I command all demons that came from that sin and (name) to leave me now in Jesus' name. I ask You to fill me with the Holy Spirit and healing and restoration for that damaged area within me in Jesus' name. (This is where you need to get two or three scriptures and pray them over yourself daily that will bring healing to that area of you and your life. It may be scriptures on holiness, or self-control, love, peace, etc. The word is alive and it will perform that good work in you.)

Chapter 5

SUDDENLY THERE WAS A GREAT EARTHQUAKE"

Acts 16:25-26 *"Around midnight, as Paul and Silas were praying and singing hymns to the Lord- and the other prisoners were listening- suddenly there was a great earthquake; the prison was shaken to its foundations, all the doors flew open - and the chains of every prisoner fell off!"* TLB

> § Every miracle in the Bible started as a problem.

We took a brief look at this scripture earlier, but I wanted you to see and understand that this is a classic example of warring with worship. Paul and Silas had been beaten for casting a demon out of a young girl who had been following them for days. This created such a stir that Paul and Silas were beaten with rods and thrown into prison. Most of us would by this time be at the very least whining to God because of the injustice that was being done to us. Paul and Silas, however, had learned to praise God no matter what their circumstances were. We all need to follow this example and get to that same place because verse twenty-six won't happen in our lives until verse twenty-five happens. We must get to the place of praying and praising God even in the worst of circumstances because we serve a miracle working God. Never forget that God can shake the circumstances that have trapped you and He can set you free as well as all those with you by the power of His Holy Spirit.

> § Trust God in the worst of circumstances and BELIEVE!

Verse twenty-five says this took place at the midnight hour. The shaking may have taken place at the midnight hour, but the praying and praising took place long before that. Another example of a really strong faith in God in all circumstances is in Job 13:15 where Job said, *"yet though You slay me, I will trust You."* Trusting God in all circumstances is a hard concept to grasp but it is necessary in order to go to the next level with God. Hebrews six reminds us it is impossible to please God without faith. Trusting God in all circumstances is exactly that: faith. I have decided to be a God pleaser and I want to pass those tests when He gives them to me so I am determined not to dwell on circumstances but on God and His trustworthiness.

Sometimes in a horse race, blinders will be placed on the horse's eyes so that they are not distracted by what's going on around them. We need to ask God to put blinders on us so that we can see Him and that

heavenly prize and that we will reach toward it. If the distractions are evil in nature they need to be rebuked, so rebuke them in Jesus' name. If they need to be cast out, then cast them out in Jesus' name. If they are just an aggravation, then turn away from them and focus on Jesus Christ and Him crucified. Focus on the promises of God and His Word and praise Him even in the midnight hour. I am determined to trust God and praise Him in the midst of adversity or personal trials, even at the midnight hour.

§
Trust is higher than faith.

Acts 12:1-12 "*Now about that time Herod the king stretched out his hand to harass some from the church. Then he killed James the brother of John with the sword. And because he saw that it pleased the Jews, he proceeded further to seize Peter also. Now it was during the Days of Unleavened Bread. So when he had apprehended him, he put him in prison, and delivered him to four squads of soldiers to keep him, intending to bring him before the people after Passover. Peter was therefore kept in prison, but* **constant prayer was offered to God for him by the church**. *And when Herod was about to bring him out, that night Peter was sleeping, bound with two chains between two soldiers; and the guards before the door were keeping the prison. Now behold, an angel of the Lord stood by him, and a light shone in the prison; and he struck Peter on the side and raised him up, saying, "Arise quickly!" And his chains fell off his hands. Then the angel said to him, "Gird yourself and tie on your sandals"; and so he did. And he said to him, "Put on your garment and follow me." So he went out and followed him, and did not know that what was done by the angel was real, but thought he was seeing a vision. When they were past the first and the second guard posts, they came to the iron gate that leads to the city, which opened to them of its own accord; and they went out and went down one street, and immediately the angel departed from him. And when Peter had come to himself, he said, "Now I know for certain that the Lord has sent His angel, and has delivered me from the hand of Herod and from all the expectation of the Jewish people." So, when he had considered this, he came to the house of Mary, the mother of John whose surname was Mark, where many were gathered together praying.*" [emphasis added]

The church and the leaders of the church were under heavy persecution. That is hard for us to understand here in America but the church is suffering persecution in many parts of this world. It looked bleak. James had been murdered and Herod's soldiers had taken Peter captive and turned him over to four squads of soldiers which meant sixteen soldiers. Peter knew that James was dead and

He was in prison with four squads of soldiers around him. If a prisoner escaped the soldiers guarding him lost their lives. So they would not have been slack to guard him.

The church did not give up because they knew God and they prayed to Him constantly on Peter's behalf. Peter needed deliverance from his enemies. The blessing would come after he got out of prison. The church was in constant prayer even at the midnight hour. Look at the last verse in the text. It says that he went to the house of Mary where many were gathered together praying. They did not give up and turn on the television or go mow the lawn, they prayed constantly. Understand that constant prayer does not mean a few simple words like, "Bless him Lord." Constant prayer is praying until God answers. How many times do we give up just before the answer gets here when we should have done as the church did for Peter, pray continually?

The Lord sent an angel who led Peter to safety when Peter had been asleep. Sometimes you get the answer praising and sometimes you can go ahead and go to sleep because the peace of God has entered your spirit and you are abiding in Him.

To give you an example from my life: we helped women coming out of prison for four years. Then my husband and I both heard that we should shut down the ministry if the finances hadn't changed by a specific date. We did end up closing this ministry. Then I called a ministry friend to pray for the sale of the building we had been using to house these women. My friend suggested we ask for the most aggressive sales person in the real-estate company that we had chosen. We had been praying about that as well and my husband and I heard the same name in our individual prayer times. So I called them and took my friend's advice and asked for the most aggressive salesman in the office. A woman called me back and set an appointment. I did not stop praying because I got the answer. I still prayed about it and took it before the Lord. The morning the agent was coming to view the property the Lord spoke to me and said the agent already had a buyer. A few minutes later my ministry friend called and said the Lord told her in prayer that the salesman already had a buyer. So when the realtor arrived to view the property I told her what God told me in prayer that morning. She immediately chimed in and assured me that she too had prayed. Then she stopped for a minute and said she did have someone who was looking for a building like ours. See, sometimes you need to war till you see the victory and sometimes as Peter did in the scripture above you can go to sleep because the victory is already yours.

> § God answered their prayers with a miracle because they had a problem!

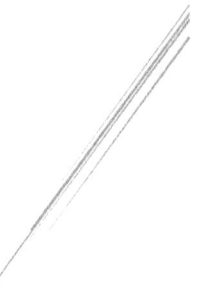

It is very important to understand which it is. Do you need to war till the victory is won or can you go to sleep because God has it covered? This is where it is absolutely critical that you have a close fellowship with the Holy Spirit so He can instruct you. If you are abiding you will hear God. Remember He is merciful and He wants us to grow up and walk with Him in the authority that He has given us.

John 15:7 "*If you abide in Me, and My words abide in you, you will ask what you desire, and it shall be done for you.*"

Abiding is not passivity. It is when you have done all you can do through prayer, worship and warfare and God brings the answer. We might have prayed that God would change Herod's heart or give Peter the strength and peace as he was being led to his execution. But God had other ideas. We might ask for an answer that we can understand, whereas God is going to answer in a way that we could never imagine. God's ways are not our ways and His thoughts are not our thoughts. So stop trying to reason God and allow Him to be God. Learn to pray, worship, and war, and leave the way He answers up to Him.

Prayer - God give us the desire to live and believe in the sudden happenings. Give us the ability to praise You in the midnight hour and to pray effectively. Let us be a church that is in constant prayer believing in a God that keeps His Word, in Jesus' name we pray. Amen.

§

Both the church and Peter had a different part to play!

§

Abiding is not passivity! When you have done all you can through prayer, worship and warfare then God will bring the answer.

1. Remember a time in your own life where God came through at that last minute. Write it down. What scripture, if any, did He give you to hang onto?

2. Find another example in the Word that depicts answered prayer when all looked hopeless.

3. Determine to pray as directed by the Holy Spirit every day. Pray also with understanding of the situation as you know it to be. What is God telling you to pray for now? Write it down. Find two or three scriptures to base the answer on and stand on God's Word.

ARE YOU FULLY PERSUADED?

Galatians 3:13-14, 29 "*Christ has redeemed us from the curse of the law, having become a curse for us (for it is written, "Cursed is everyone who hangs on a tree"), that the blessing of Abraham might come upon the Gentiles in Christ Jesus, that we might receive the promise of the Spirit through faith. 29 And if you are Christ's, then you are Abraham's seed, and heirs according to the promise.*"

The blessing of Abraham is the covenant that was made between him and God.

Genesis 15:7-21 "*Then He said to him, "I am the LORD, who brought you out of Ur of the Chaldeans, to give you this land to inherit it." And he said, "Lord GOD, how shall I know that I will inherit it?" So He said to him, "Bring Me a three-year-old heifer, a three-year-old female goat, a three-year-old ram, a turtledove, and a young pigeon." Then he brought all these to Him and cut them in two, down the middle, and placed each piece opposite the other; but he did not cut the birds in two. And when the vultures came down on the carcasses, Abram drove them away. Now when the sun was going down, a deep sleep fell upon Abram; and behold, horror and great darkness fell upon him. Then He said to Abram: "Know certainly that your descendants will be strangers in a land that is not theirs, and will serve them, and they will afflict them four hundred years. And also the nation whom they serve I will judge; afterward they shall come out with great possessions. Now as for you, you shall go to your fathers in peace; you shall be buried at a good old age. But in the fourth generation they shall return here, for the iniquity of the Amorites is not yet complete." And it came to pass, when the sun went down and it was dark, that behold, there appeared a smoking oven and a burning torch that passed between those pieces. On the same day the LORD made a covenant with Abram, saying: "To your descendants I have given this land, from the river of Egypt to the great river, the River Euphrates--the Kenites, the Kenezzites, and the Kadmonites, the Hittites, the Perizzites, and the Rephaim, the Amorites, the Canaanites, the Girgashites, and the Jebusites.*"

§ God cut a covenant by the blood of an animal.

A covenant is a binding contract. God established the contract on both sides. God knew that man could not keep this type of contract. Only God could assume responsibility for the administration of this covenant.

The cutting in half signifies the ending of two separate lives and establishes that a new bond or covenant was being made between God

> § Later the covenant would be by the blood of His Son!

and man. This was a sacred bond because there was the shedding of blood. Since this covenant was initiated by God and a blood sacrifice was offered, which was a requirement for this contract, it rested completely on God. As you can see from the text God and Jesus walked between the pieces as represented by a smoking oven and a burning torch passing between the pieces.

In an ancient Hittite covenant the inferior leader would walk between the pieces taking an oath to his superior. "May the gods do so to me (and more also) as I have done to these animals if I do not fulfill the terms of this covenant." The Bible is not a Western book but an Eastern Book. So Abram knew what a covenant was because he lived in an Eastern culture. The Lord made Himself lower than Abram to establish this covenant. This dramatic act portrays what He would do later when He gave His son Jesus to die on a cross as a perfect sacrifice. The covenant was proposed by God, was made by God, and was guaranteed by God. Remember, Abram was asleep. Nothing was required of Abram except to believe it and receive it.

What God was saying when He made the covenant with and for Abram was "everything I have is yours, and everything you have is Mine." Under the new covenant which was initiated by God and sealed by the blood of Jesus through His death, burial and resurrection our sins were forgiven. Not only were our sins forgiven but our salvation was instituted and our destination was changed from hell to heaven. By faith we are saved and through that sacrifice of blood our covenant was sealed with the perfection of Jesus Christ. Jesus came to save the lost, heal the sick and set the captive free. His blood seals a new covenant promise that when I cry out to Him for salvation He hears and saves me; also, that when I am sick, He will send forth His word with healing. (Psalm 107:20) God desires for me to be free of the captivity that has been orchestrated by the devil. Jesus was the perfect blood sacrifice that was provided for you and me and our document of proof is the Word of God. The Bible is God's contract to you so that you know without a doubt what He has provided for you. Everything God has is mine and all I have to do is hand Him my diseases, sickness, poverty, sin, transgressions, iniquities and receive back from Him salvation, healing, prosperity, forgiveness, freedom. I also get to be filled with the power of the Holy Spirit to help me walk out this life in victory. Hallelujah!

Hebrews 6:13-15 *"For when God made a promise to Abraham, because He could swear by no one greater, He swore by Himself, saying, "Surely*

blessing I will bless you, and multiplying I will multiply you." And so, after he had patiently endured, he obtained the promise."

God swore by Himself because He could swear by no one greater, so when He says, *"Surely blessing I will bless you, and multiplying I will multiply you"*, God has sworn by Himself and we can believe that what Jesus accomplished on the cross is for us today and believe and receive the covenant made with him which was initiated by God, performed by God, and was guaranteed by God.

Romans 4:21 *"And being fully persuaded that what He had promised, He was able also to perform."* KJV

Prayer - Father make me a man or woman that is fully persuaded, in Jesus' name.

§
God cannot lie!

1. What is a covenant?

2. How is a covenant made and sealed?

3. Find a scripture in the New Testament that refers to the better covenant that we have in Christ.

4. What does God want you to receive now because of this covenant?

Blessed be the Lord, Who daily loads us with benefits, the God of our salvation!" **Psalm 68:19**

Matthew 8:17 "*that it might be fulfilled which was spoken by Isaiah the prophet, saying: "He Himself took our infirmities and bore our sicknesses."*

This scripture states that Jesus took our infirmities or diseases and He bore our sickness. This is a very specific verse. Either God is who He says He is and He'll do what He said He'll do, or He is a liar. *"God is not a man, that He should lie".* (Numbers 23:19) It is also stated in Titus chapter one, the second verse that *"God cannot lie."* God desires for us to be healed and there are many scriptures that prove this promise is for us and for today.

1 Peter 2:24 "*Who Himself bore our sins in His own body on the tree, that we, having died to sins, might live for righteousness--by whose stripes you were healed."*

This was written in past tense because this was done on the cross by Jesus so the healing has already been done. We are to believe and receive our healings. In my own case the Lord told me that He was healing me of chronic bronchitis. I was on a high dose of medication for that lung condition but I had a word from God. The Lord told me that I was going to preach and at that time I did not have enough lung capacity to speak for a long period of time. I was painting my son's room and I heard the Lord clearly tell me that He was healing me of chronic bronchitis and He told me to sing as loud and long as I could every day before I went to work. My lungs and my diaphragm muscles were healed and at the end of the year I no longer needed the medication.

There was another time right after I was totally surrendered to the Holy Spirit that my husband woke up about two in the morning very sick. He had a high fever and I could hear that his lungs were very congested. I was a respiratory therapist and I knew that he needed to go to the hospital right away. My husband was also a bad asthmatic but he refused to go and took something for the fever and came back to bed. As soon as his head touched the pillow he fell into a deep sleep. The Lord spoke to me very clearly to put one hand on his head and one on his chest and receive his healing for him. We were in a denominational church and I can remember telling the Lord that Larry was going to be so mad when he got healed because our church did not believe in it. I did not even question that he would be healed because I had heard God and had a word from God.

§ God desires for us to be healed.

This was so new to me and I did not even know if I could receive someone's healing for them but God did. So I did what he told me to do and then I went to sleep. Three hours later my husband woke up and said, "I feel great, my chest is clear, no fever but I still have a sore throat." He never told me that his throat was sore. I just chuckled thinking that if I grabbed him by the throat he would never believe that I was praying for a healing. When he woke up at seven he looked at me and said, "You prayed for me didn't you?" I nodded wondering if he was going to blow up but he did not. In fact, he never said anything about it until a few weeks later.

He was not only healed from possible pneumonia but he was also healed of asthma and he has never taken any medication to this day which has been a number of years. He got more than I prayed for but isn't that like God?

James 5:14-16 "*Is anyone among you sick? Let him call for the elders of the church, and let them pray over him, anointing him with oil in the name of the Lord. And the prayer of faith will save the sick, and the Lord will raise him up. And if he has committed sins, he will be forgiven. Confess your trespasses to one another, and pray for one another, that you may be healed. The effective, fervent prayer of a righteous man avails much.*"

This scripture verifies that sickness can also come from sin. But what are we to do? The scriptures say to call for the elders, anoint with oil, and believe, which is to have faith in God that His Word is true. Then God will raise up the sick and forgive the sinner so that they may be healed. Our prayers are very important if prayed correctly. Scripturally correct prayers are effective prayers. Please quit praying if it be God's will. His Word is His will. Praying correctly and with passion works, but do not forget the part of the sentence that uses the word 'righteous'.

I do understand that many of you reading this book do not have elders in your church that believe this scripture. They really only believe in what they can see, touch and understand. But there are godly people who do believe either in your congregation or a different one, seek them out and ask them to pray and agree with you for your healing. Please don't not go to the doctor, medicine is creative and there are godly, good doctors who can help you with this as well. I do both, I pray for healing and I go to the doctor and continue in prayer until the problem is corrected, either physically or supernaturally.

§
Scripturally correct prayers are effective prayers.

Psalm 35:27 *"Let the LORD be magnified, Who has pleasure in the prosperity of His servant."*

Psalm 68:6 ..."*He brings out those who are bound into prosperity;*"

3 John 2-4 *"Beloved, I pray that you may prosper in all things and be in health, just as your soul prospers. For I rejoiced greatly when brethren came and testified of the truth that is in you, just as you walk in the truth. I have no greater joy than to hear that my children walk in truth."*

§ Hebrews 13:8 *Jesus is the same yesterday, today and forever.*

The apostle John states in the last verse that we should prosper in all things: that is physically, spiritually, socially and financially. This is walking in truth. We can deny the truth but that does not mean that it is not true, maybe it is just not true to us. I have lived too many years hearing pastors explain away the miracles in the book of Acts and that is not God. That is man's doctrine. The truth is the Word and until we get a handle on it and believe it, we will spend our lives saved, but defeated. Been there done that and I'm not going back, hallelujah!

God wants us saved, filled with His Spirit, delivered, healthy, and blessed financially. What father does not want the best for his children, and God is a perfect Father. This does not mean that we won't have trials but we can have victory and fulfill the mission that God has for us.

Malachi 3:10 *"Bring all the tithes into the storehouse, that there may be food in My house, And try Me now in this,"* Says the LORD of hosts, *"If I will not open for you the windows of heaven and pour out for you such blessing that there will not be room enough to receive it."*

If you are tithing and giving offerings and this is not happening then break off a curse of poverty and command all demons associated with that curse to leave in the name of Jesus. Thank God every day for rebuking the devourer for your sake and pouring out an enormous blessing. It would have to be enormous if we would not have room enough to receive it. Now, if you are not tithing, then you are in disobedience. Begin to tithe, which is ten percent of your gross income. If that is too much at first, start with five percent and work your way up. God is merciful. He can see your heart. Ask for forgiveness and if there are any demons afflicting you because of your disobedience, command them to leave in Jesus' name.

Prayer - Father, teach me Your Word and let me believe and receive what You have for me, not what man has taught me. I want to be a believer and a receiver in Jesus' name.

1. Find a scripture in the New Testament about healing besides the ones in this lesson. Write it down.

2. Have you ever prayed for healing? What happened? [Infirmity and Unclean spirits can bring many sicknesses. Command them out then receive your healing.]

3. Find another scripture on prosperity in the Old or New Testament and write it down.

4. What must you do to align yourself with God's Word about healing and prosperity?

PRAY WITH AN UNDERSTANDING OF GOD'S WORD

Jeremiah 33:3 *"Call to Me, and I will answer you, and show you great and mighty things, which you do not know."*

When God began to teach me to pray, I knew very little about prayer. When I did pray it never seemed to work so I needed help. The Lord gave me this verse in Jeremiah and then He began to teach me as I studied His Word. Also, as I began my daily time with Him, I would sense the Holy Spirit leading me to a particular verse. Then I would hear in my mind to pray that scripture over the person for whom I had been praying as He would then quicken my heart to pray that scripture.

When I went into the Christian bookstore the Lord would also tell me which books to buy. I knew very little about the Holy Spirit although I had been saved for nine years. We were in a denominational church that preached salvation every week to a room full of saved people. But God is faithful and as I began to learn to pray and pray with an understanding of God's Word, I started to see answers. Then God began to lead me to pray for specific people and to pray a certain way. In some cases, He told me things that I was not privy to but I prayed just as He directed me. Sometimes I heard a testimony at the new church that we were going to that was exactly what I had prayed. I was ecstatic. Because I prayed a lot for myself, I began to change dramatically. Thank you Jesus I needed to change. I prayed scripture over myself. I declared God's Word over myself and not only could I and my family see the difference, but those I worked with could as well.

I am filled with the Holy Spirit and I operate in all the gifts of the Holy Spirit as the Spirit wills for the good of the body, the word of wisdom, word of knowledge, discerning of spirits of good and evil, prophecy, diverse kinds of tongues, and interpretation of tongues, the gift of faith, the working of miracles, and the gifts of healings, in Jesus' name. (1 Corinthians 12:7-11)

I believe that God is rewarding me because I diligently seek Him. (Hebrews 11:6)

I am wise and I listen and increase in learning. (Proverbs 1:5)

I thank You, Father that I trust in You and not my own understanding. I acknowledge You in all my ways and You are directing my path. (Proverbs 3:5-6)

§
In order to pray with authority, you must know what the Authority says in His Word.

No shortcuts.

Wisdom is found on my lips because I have understanding and I store up knowledge. (Proverbs 10:13-14)

Counselors of peace have joy, and I am a counselor of peace and I have joy. (Proverbs 12:20b)

I am a faithful ambassador and I bring healing. (Proverbs 13:17b)

I answer softly and I turn away wrath. I have a wholesome tongue and it brings life. (Proverbs 15:1a, 4a)

I open my mouth with wisdom and the law of kindness is in my tongue. (Proverbs 31:26)

God has created in me a clean heart and renewed that steadfast spirit within me. (Psalm 51:10)

I have a spirit of power and love and a sound mind. I do not have a spirit of fear. (2 Timothy 1:7)

I am increasing in wisdom, stature and favor with God and men. (Luke 2:52)

I think on things which are true, noble, just, pure, lovely, of good report as well as meditating on virtuous and praiseworthy things in Jesus' name. (Philippians 4:8)

I seek those thing which are above and set my mind not on the things of the earth. My life is hidden with Christ in God therefore I put away all filthiness from me in Jesus' name. (Colossians 3:1-9)

These are just a few of the scriptures that I prayed over myself every day. I had a list of about 150 scriptures and I prayed these scriptures every day in my prayer time. I needed a lot of work. But praise God the Word works. As I spoke those scriptures over myself they became true. I did some for my husband and our sons and I saw big improvement within a few weeks in them as well. I first bound the evil that I saw was on me and then on my husband and sons. I did not know then that I could command them to leave. I learned that later and then I took all of us through prayers of deliverance.

You must begin to learn God's Word because God's Word is His will. As God taught me to pray, I learned to use scriptures because in Isaiah the Bible says that God's Word will not return void but it will accomplish that thing that it was sent to do. God's Word is alive and able to save, deliver, heal, change us, and give us hope.

> § God's Word is alive and able to save, deliver, heal, change us, and give us hope.

In order to pray with authority, you have to know what the Authority says in His Word. There are no short cuts. Get excited about the Holy Spirit and a life of daily surrender to a God who has plans for us for good and not for evil. Amen.

Prayer - Father teach me to pray, to pray to get results that will bear fruit so that fruit will remain. Give me the strength to surrender, the courage to be obedient and the wisdom to die to self. In Your Son's name I pray.

1. Do you know how to pray?

2. What is God telling you to do to change your prayer life or begin one?

3. Write out several scriptures that you need to say over yourself every day. [Proverbs and Psalms are full of scriptures that will change you forever.]

4. Write out the Scriptures that God is telling you to say over your family or friends.

5. Write a prayer either for a need in your life or a loved one's life. [Start with praising God, then get the demons bound away, then state your request. End with thanksgiving.]

Chapter 6

"MY PEOPLE ARE DESTROYED FOR LACK OF KNOWLEDGE."

Ephesians 6:12-18 *"For we do not wrestle against flesh and blood, but against principalities, against powers, against the rulers of the darkness of this age, against spiritual hosts of wickedness in the heavenly places. Therefore take up the whole armor of God that you may be able to withstand in the evil day, and having done all, to stand. Stand therefore, having girded your waist with truth, having put on the breastplate of righteousness, and having shod your feet with the preparation of the gospel of peace; above all, taking the shield of faith with which you will be able to quench all the fiery darts of the wicked one. And take the helmet of salvation, and the sword of the Spirit, which is the word of God; praying always with all prayer and supplication in the Spirit, being watchful to this end with all perseverance and supplication for all the saints."*

We do not fight against flesh and blood. I hope that you understand that. We war in the heavenlies. Your spouse or children are not bad but demonized (assaulted by demons). Get them free in prayer and you will see them free in this natural world.

There is no way to withstand in this evil day without the armor of God. The whole armor is not just our footwear. So many churches spread the gospel of peace and stop there without including the other pieces God gave us. The shoes are not all there is.

When we gird our waist with truth, we put on the whole Word of God not just the parts we like or make us feel comfortable. The truth is Jesus and Jesus did not just preach the gospel. The truth is preaching the gospel, healing the sick, casting out demons and raising the dead. That is what we are to do not pick out what we like and leave the rest. This book is to teach you about God so that you can form a love relationship with Him and have it on a much deeper level. That is called **worship**. This book is also to teach you about the enemy and how to fight him. That is called **warfare**. You must be a seeker of truth which will make you a seeker of Jesus because *"He is the way, the truth, and the life."* (John 14:6) **If you cannot recognize the truth then you will fall to a lie.**

§
There is no way to withstand in this evil day without the whole armor of God.

§
The Shoes of Peace

§
The Belt of Truth

§
The Breastplate
of Righteousness

§
Don't be in the wrong place at the wrong time!

§
Go where God sends you and do what He tells you to do.

§
If you're ignorant of the workings of the devil, he will take advantage of you.

The next piece of armor is the breastplate of righteousness. This was done on the cross by Jesus. His sacrifice made us righteous because only blood could atone for sin. If we have accepted Him as our Savior, Jesus atoned for our sin forever. Salvation puts on that breastplate of righteousness. So as you put that on each day as you put on the rest of the armor, realize Jesus is righteous and we are in Him. We can all make wrong choices but God has given us the armor of God for our protection as well as for offensive as we fight the enemy and spread the light of Jesus Christ in a lost and dying world.

King David who was a worshiper and a warrior also found himself in the wrong place at the wrong time just like many of us have. David was a worshiper and a warrior but he fell into sin with Bathsheba. Did he love God? Absolutely. Did God love him? Absolutely. God called him a man after His own heart. Did he fall into a trap set by the devil? Yes, and it cost him dearly.

2 Samuel 11:1-2 *"It happened in the spring of the year, at the time when kings go out to battle, that David sent Joab and his servants with him, and all Israel; and they destroyed the people of Ammon and besieged Rabbah. But David remained at Jerusalem. Then it happened one evening that David arose from his bed and walked on the roof of the king's house. And from the roof he saw a woman bathing, and the woman was very beautiful to behold."*

David was king and he should have been warring. He was not alert to the enemy of our souls. He was in the wrong season. He was resting when he should have been at war with his men and he paid a very big price for his sin. There is a time for everything in our lives and God doesn't want us to miss His timing because we have chosen to do our own thing. Because of David being in the wrong place at the wrong time, he fell into sin with Bathsheba. He had Bathsheba's husband put in the front of the battle to be killed and then David lost two sons because he did not recognize the traps of the enemy.

2 Corinthians 2:11 *"... lest Satan should take advantage of us; for we are not ignorant of his devices."*

Satan can take advantage of us when we are ignorant of his schemes. I pray quite often for God to reveal to me the traps that Satan is laying for me and my family. I want to stop the enemy far away before he harms any of us.

The moral of the story of King David and Bathsheba is not to be in the wrong place at the wrong time. Instead be where God wants you to be.

Ask the Lord to set in you that inner alarm that will go off when you are getting away from His Word or uncomfortable in His presence. Unconfessed sin will make you uncomfortable in God's presence. But there is a time to worship and a time to war. Those that worship and never leave the throne room are like the early priests who never disciplined their families or kept the enemy off them. Eli's sons were wicked and were destroyed. Two of Aaron's sons were killed for offering strange fire in the Holy of Holies.

§ War AND worship.

Warring alone will make you focus on the devil instead of God. The blend is to go from worship to warfare and back again. I always have a sense of worship about me even when I sense the enemy. I learned to worship first and it is so ingrained in me that it has become a part of me. Then the Lord taught me the tactics of the enemy. I try never to forget that order because as surely as I do, I'll get off. I have missed it a few times when the attacks were so great and seemed to be coming from all directions. But praise God He never let me get too far off and when I wandered out too far, He corrected me. The reason He could correct me is because I love the Word. It is in my heart and mind. This is such an essential part of your spiritual growth.

Ask God to reveal Satan's traps to you every day so that you and your loved ones can walk in victory.

Prayer - Dear Lord, make me aware of the war and let me see your glory and taste your victory and fight the good fight of faith until my days are over. In Jesus' name I pray.

1. How does Satan take advantage of us? Give an example other than the one used in this lesson.

2. How has the devil harmed you and your family? Write it out, starting with yourself.

3. Now that you can see the enemy's traps ask God to show you how to devise a prayer plan to destroy the works of the enemy. What are your first steps? Write them down starting with yourself.

FAITH IS THE VICTORY THAT OVERCOMES THE WORLD

Ephesians 6:16-17 *"above all, taking the shield of faith with which you will be able to quench all the fiery darts of the wicked one. And take the helmet of salvation, and the sword of the Spirit, which is the word of God;"*

§ Why first the Shield of Faith?

Why would the Shield of Faith be above all? First of all, you cannot even get saved without faith. Faith is daring to go beyond what the eyes see. You cannot see Jesus but He speaks to your heart. You cannot touch His hand but you can trust Him. You cannot look into His eyes to see the truth but you can look in His Word and know it is truth. Faith is believing and receiving and going beyond what your natural eyes can see.

Hebrews 11:6 *"But without faith it is impossible to please Him, for he who comes to God must believe that He is, and that He is a rewarder of those who diligently seek Him."*

This is such a simple verse but yet so weighty. For years the church has operated with faith for salvation and that is it. But God says there is more. Salvation is the <u>first</u> step not the <u>only</u> step, because as you surrender completely to the Holy Spirit and immerse yourself into God and the things of God, you will begin to understand faith.

The Shield of Faith quenches all the fiery darts of the wicked one. If you are not in faith, then you are in fear. Fear is not from God. Rebuke it and line yourself back up with God's Word and put up that Shield of Faith. Cry out God's Word! When I sense attacks, I speak out of my mouth that I am putting up the Shield of Faith which puts out or quenches all the fiery darts in the name of Jesus. Hallelujah! I can literally feel the enemy pull away from me and whatever I am praying for.

I try to stay alert at all times. I have asked God to wake me up in the night if any of us or anyone we are connected to goes under attack. I also ask Him to show me the traps of the enemy while I am awake. If I go somewhere and fear comes on me, it is not mine so I look around to see what's going on. I also ask the Lord to show me what cannot be seen with human eyes but to open my spiritual eyes to the spiritual war. Then I attack the enemy and like a smart bomb, it goes to the correct target and does no collateral damage. In other words, the prayer accomplishes what it was sent to accomplish because it is God's Word spoken by God's child doing God's will. Hallelujah! I cannot help but shout even when I write.

§ Helmet of Salvation

The scripture then mentions a Helmet of Salvation. That Helmet covers your mind, personality, all that makes you who you are. The Helmet is the saving knowledge of Jesus Christ and it is also the Word because Jesus is the Word. In order to protect your head and brain in battle you wear a helmet. The helmet must cover adequately what it is meant to protect and it must be sturdy enough to withstand blows to the head and neck area.

In ancient times the helmets went down almost to the shoulder and also covered the ears. This protects your brain where your mind is centered. This is where you make decisions and make choices. This is where your personality is centered and your uniqueness of character. The neck can be broken easily by a trained soldier and the helmet covers that exposed area. The ears are covered as well. If you have filled your mind with the Word of God and have covered your ears to the negativity of the world then Satan has no entry point to attack you.

§ Sword of the Spirit

Always be vigilant and surround yourself with faith then as you pray you are wielding the Sword of the Spirit, which is the Word of God. That Sword is destroying the works of the enemy and replacing them with God's Word which is His will. If you know God's Word, then you know His will. That Sword will bring the light to a dark situation because Jesus is the Word. *"He was clothed with a robe dipped in blood, and His name is called The Word of God."* (Revelation 19:13)

§ Jesus is the Word.

Jesus is also called the light of the world. He is the Word and He is the Sword because He was in the beginning. *"In the beginning was the Word, and the Word was with God, and the Word was God. He was in the beginning with God. All things were made through Him, and without Him nothing was made that was made. In Him was life, and the life was the light of men. And the light shines in the darkness, and the darkness did not comprehend it."* (John 1:1-5) The Sword is the Word and He was in the beginning with God. Take that Word and learn how to use it as a Sword which destroys the darkness and brings the light of Christ into every situation.

Satan cannot destroy you unless you let him. He can harass you, but if he doesn't then it is because you were no threat to him before. Be a threat! Gird yourself with Truth, put on the Breastplate of Righteousness which covers your heart. Ask to be a person with an undivided heart. Put on the Shoes of the Gospel of Peace, lift up the Shield of Faith and stop the enemy. Take that Helmet of Salvation and fill your mind with the Word of God. Protect your ears and eyes from the enemy of negativity and lust. Then grab hold of the Sword of the

Spirit and pray with all types of prayer for you, your loved ones, and those that God puts in your path. Pray for your church leadership, the leadership of your country, state, and city.

Seek to become a person after God's own heart. Learn to worship and to war and commit once and for all to the army of God. You are not to be a mercenary out there all alone. You are in God's army. God has given us other believers who will encourage us and walk alongside us.

Fighting is an action word not a passive word. Faith is an action word not a passive word. Salvation, deliverance, healing are action words not passive words. Get a revelation that your circumstance and loved ones will change in prayer as you speak out loud the Word of God and war and defeat the enemy in your daily life. In order to be an affective warrior, you must die on the Sword of the Spirit first which means to die daily. You will never live to your fullest until you have died to your flesh. Amen, so be it in my life.

Prayer - Dear God, open my eyes that I might see. Open my ears that I might hear You and give me the strength and determination to learn Your Word, to fill my mind with You and change my view of warfare so that I do not see this as an attack from You or a weakness of my character but an assault by the enemy. In the name of Jesus I pray.

> §
> If you recognize the Truth of the Lord Jesus and His Word then you will recognize the works of the devil.

1. What is the armor and what is it for? What pieces have you used well and what have you used halfheartedly or never put on?

2. What is God telling you to do immediately and long range?

PRAY WITHOUT CEASING

Matthew 6:6 *"But you, when you pray, go into your room, and when you have shut your door, pray to your Father who is in the secret place; and your Father who sees in secret will reward you openly."*

God has a plan and purpose for your life and the lives of your loved ones. I prayed for myself first then my husband then our sons. I did this in my prayer time. I did not tell them that I was praying the evil off and replacing it with the good. They never heard me pray this way for them until much later when they were in the midst of change and desiring to change more by the power of the Holy Spirit. I went to the secret place with God and learned to pray, to seek him, to fight in the spirit for myself and my family. I sought Him in the secret place and He rewarded me openly, or in the natural realm. Your mouth will not change anyone if it is not changed first. Get your mouth saved and spirit-filled and speak out the words of God.

§ Your mouth will not change anyone if it is not changed first.

When I see answered prayer, I then ask God what to pray for next. I always expect to see the answer. Some things take longer than others. James 5:16 says the effectual and fervent prayer of a righteous man works. Pray with passion and effectively.

§ Ask God what to pray and how to pray. EXPECT AN ANSWER

1 Thessalonians 5:16-19 *"Rejoice always, pray without ceasing, in everything give thanks; for this is the will of God in Christ Jesus for you. Do not quench the Spirit."*

Be ever filled with joy, never stop praying and give thanks **in** everything not **for** everything. Some have taught that we are to thank God for all the bad things that threaten to destroy. **Not so!** The scripture says to give thanks **in** everything. I can give thanks to God while I am going through the trial such as Paul and Silas did in the prison. We can give thanks and praise to God in the midst of the trial but the beatings come from the devil and those that he controls.

§ Do not quench the Spirit!

"Do not quench the Spirit!" Do not deny His existence, His power, and His effectiveness to turn a Peter who denied Christ three times into a Peter that preached and thousands were saved and the church was added to daily. You need to be filled with the Holy Spirit so that you are sensitive to Him and can pray as you are led by the Spirit to pray. We are to be vigilant in prayer, to quit thinking that everything that runs through our head is us. If it is sin then it is not God and if we have turned our hearts toward God and we do not desire what we can see in our mind then it is not us. That leaves the devil so the field has narrowed. The next thing you need to determine is if it is coming at you

because of a weakness you haven't dealt with or is someone you know under attack. Or maybe it is the devil attacking you to see if he can lure you into sin. I do not take the rap for Satan throwing trash into my mind, I rebuke him. If it does not leave, then I ask God if there is something I need to take care of. If I determine that neither of those are correct then I begin to ask God who does He want me to intercede for in prayer.

Job 22:30 "*He will even deliver the one [for whom you intercede] who is not innocent; yes, he will be delivered through the cleanness of your hands.*" AMPC

Prayer is not just a list of people or places. It's sensitivity to the Holy Spirit so that God's Word is declared over that person or situation until it is changed by the power of His Spirit.

§
God wants to use you.

Paul started all of his letters with a greeting and then he always spoke of his prayers for them. Take a look at Philippians 1:3-6 where Paul writes, "*I thank my God upon every remembrance of you, always in every prayer of mine for you all making request with joy, for your fellowship in the gospel from the first day until now; being confident of this very thing, that He which hath begun a good work in you will perform it until the day of Jesus Christ.*" KJV

Paul never gave up. He never became disgusted and quit, he kept on keeping on. He believed, as we should, that God will perform that good work because it is God's Word and His Will. He trusted God and he prayed with understanding. Do not give up. Just believe that as you pray in secret, effectively, as well as passionately, that God will reward your prayers openly.

Romans 8:26-27 "*Likewise the Spirit also helps in our weaknesses. For we do not know what we should pray for as we ought, but the Spirit Himself makes intercession for us with groanings which cannot be uttered. Now He who searches the hearts knows what the mind of the Spirit is, because He makes intercession for the saints according to the will of God.*"

Prayer - Help me, Lord to pray passionately and effectively. Teach me to know You and Your Word. Give me a heart of prayer and a mind that is open to You but not fooled by the traps of the enemy. Bring me up to a new level in worship, warfare and faith. In Jesus' name I pray.

1. Have you learned to pray without ceasing?

2. Have you seen any changes in the way you pray since you started this prayer series?

3. How does God want you to change the way you pray?

"Enlarge the place of your tent"

Isaiah 54:2-3 *"Enlarge the place of your tent, and let them stretch out the curtains of your dwellings; do not spare; lengthen your cords, and strengthen your stakes. For you shall expand to the right and to the left."*

What you did last year is not good enough for this year. If you have learned more about worship and warfare and you are seeing and understanding better than you ever have then ask God to give you new territory and battle strategies.

Your ministry must always begin at home but then it is time to see your territory enlarged. Your sphere of influence and scope of ministry must enlarge as you move on with God. This scripture in Isaiah speaks of enlarging your sphere of influence. Where your tent is located is where you are. It starts out with enlarging your tent. You may fit in your tent quite comfortably. However, Jesus did not come to make us comfortable. A few years back it seemed as if every time I was moving and touching all around me that God threw in something unexpected. I thought I knew what God wanted me to do and how He wanted me to do it and then the scenery changed. I had to enlarge my vision. The curtains or what I could see and touch got bigger the stakes or the influence that I had was getting longer and unmanageable. Praise God! When I cannot manage then God moves in.

The Lord put me on a fast track of learning for five years which strengthened my stakes. Then He began to expand me to the left and to the right. When God begins to expand sometimes it can make religious people mad. I wasn't too crazy about that part but praise God He is persistent and I was desperate for Him and all that He had for me to do. I stayed focused on the cross. Sometimes I had to leave people behind. Other times people just didn't want to go where God was taking me. It was either too hard on them and their families or they just didn't want a life set aside for God. It does require commitment.

Now as I see things begin to take shape, I begin to look around to see if God is opening new territory and with every new territory comes new battle strategies. God is the one that leads me not my hopes or my desires but His. Because my heart's desire is to please the Father, I have learned to have no agenda of my own, but to be led by the Holy Spirit. God has not taken me on an erratic course. He is a builder. Remember He created the earth in an orderly yet magnificent way. He will do the same for you as He expands your territory.

§
How does God want you to enlarge the place of your tent?

Years ago, I read a book by Evelyn Christianson, "What Happens When Women Pray". She explained that when God answers a prayer the answer you get may not be the answer. What comes next may be the answer. Isaac was an answer to prayer for Abraham and Sarah but the real answer was not just Isaac but what came next. Abraham was to be the father of many nations and Isaac was an answer but look at what came next. Abraham was the father of the Jews, God's children, and then he became the father of all Christendom.

> § What comes next may be the answer.

Learn to be content but not stuck in a rut. God's people perish without a vision. If you can see it and manage it that is your vision not God's. God's vision is much bigger than we are with far too many variables and challenges. That is how you know it belongs to God. Think about Moses. He just knew that he was supposed to go back to Egypt and lead out God's children. He didn't know the details. That is so good and so God because if he had known the details he might have turned around and gone back to bondage.

> § Small things are important because everything has a beginning.

Small things are important because everything has a beginning. "*Do not despise small beginnings,*" which is a paraphrase of Zechariah 4:10. What if Abraham had said, "One son? How can one son be a nation?" "*Do not despise small beginnings.*" The Lord did not give me a vision for ministry until I had been totally surrendered to the Holy Spirit for one and a half years. Then He spoke to me over a two to three-week period every day about the call that He had on my life. It scared me so badly that I refused for two weeks until I couldn't stand it any longer. I repented and humbly agreed to whatever He wanted me to do. If I had seen some of what has happened already, I would have really been scared. I saw a big vision that encompassed a world-wide ministry with prayer, preaching, teaching, miracles, and I heard the word deliverance. I was in a denominational church that didn't teach about deliverance and I did not know what that was. I just said "yes". I have had an exciting time and I know much is still to be fulfilled. I have a far vision. What I thought was five years away is still coming after a number of years but God is faithful. His timetable is perfect. Mine is not. I have learned to be content and follow the Lord not try to lead Him.

Remember the scriptures that spoke of David not going out to war when he should have? He missed his season and he had left God's timetable for his own. That is a very dangerous place to be because when you have missed God's season or His desire for you, you are in a place which is very vulnerable to demonic attack.

When Esther went to the king's palace she went into a new season. If she had missed this season change that God led her into, she would not have been in a place to save her people. She would have missed her destiny. I was forty when I received the vision from God for this ministry. God can do a lot in a short period of time with someone who will completely surrender and come into obedience. I was a little slow but not stupid thank You Jesus. I surrendered to His vision for me and to the best of my knowledge I have done what He has asked me to do. Sometimes I miss it but I ask for forgiveness and go back. On occasion I have whined but I am not a whiner by nature so that has not trapped me like it has some people. God is merciful and He is looking for people to just absolutely surrender and become obedient unto Him.

Another example is Elisha. When he picked up the mantle of Elijah he went into a new season. God had prepared him but still Elisha had to pick up the mantle and use it. Before he took it up, he ripped off his clothes or took off the old season, and put on the new one. He had to be ready to immediately follow God. As soon as Elisha walked away with the mantle of Elijah a miracle was required of him. 2 Kings 2:8 tells us he smote, or struck, the waters of the Jordan with his cloak and the waters parted and he walked across. When God says it is time you had better have let Him trained you because a miracle is going to be required. I have already lived a nominal Christian life. I am not interested in that. I want all that God has for me. You should, too.

With new territory or a new season come new strategies. They are God planned and all you have to do is be ready. Allow God to teach you and groom you for what comes next and believe God

Prayer - Oh Father, let me hear Your voice and seek Your face. Teach me and guide me into the way that You would have me go. Give me a diligent heart to seek You and a determined heart to walk out this destiny. Give me the ability to see a new season as it approaches so that I stay close to You as Elisha did with Elijah. Give me the understanding to take off the clothes of the old season and put on the mantle of the new season. Let me smite the waters and see a miracle. In Jesus' name I pray.

§
With new territory or a new season come new strategies.

1. Is the Lord leading you into new territory?

2. What is your responsibility? What is God's responsibility?

3. Write out a prayer and ask God to let you recognize the enemy at all levels.

4. Write a prayer that includes putting on the pieces of armor and their purpose for yourself and your loved ones.

5. Write a prayer for God to prepare you for new territory and new battle strategies.

Chapter 7

"I believed therefore I spoke." 2 Corinthians 4:13

1 John 5: 4 *"For whatever is born of God overcomes the world. And this is the victory that has overcome the world--our **faith**."*

We have already established earlier in this book that without faith you cannot please God. Faith is daring the soul [mind, will, emotions, personality] to go beyond what your eyes can see. We have a rock in our home with that saying on it. As I was writing this study I called out to my husband for a good, easy definition of faith. He was sitting at the kitchen table and turned around and looked on the shelf where the rock sat and gave me that definition. I like it and it is true. If you can see it and it is within your natural capabilities and talents then it is something you can achieve on your own. God wants us to trust Him and allow Him to give us His vision which is seen from heaven down not earth up. He wants us to just agree and allow Him to prepare us for what is coming

Romans 4:17 *"(as it is written, "I have made you a father of many nations") "in the presence of Him whom he believed--God, who gives life to the dead and calls those things which do not exist as though they did."*

Calling those things that don't exist as though they did will make some people uncomfortable because it stretches the limits of their faith. That is a good thing. God wants us to stretch out to Him but not for Him to make the vision manageable for us. This verse is used a lot by people of absolute faith. Abraham had to call himself the father of many nations just so that his faith would be built up. *"Out of the heart the mouth speaks."* (Matthew 12:34) God was preparing a man to become the father of many nations. What your mouth says, you believe. I had to declare that I would be a preacher, writer, and the head of a ministry. I said what God told me to say. At first, I would apologize about it then finally I learned to just speak it out. I am not here to convince anyone else. That is God's job. I am here to do my Father's will. He said speak it, I speak it. He said learn this, I did. He said go there, I went. I have to call those things that be not as though they are because they are more real than what I can see with my natural eyes.

§
Be a believer.

§
Faith is daring the soul to go beyond what the eyes can see.

§
Ask God to show you His will from heaven down not earth up.

When Samuel went to anoint a king, Jessie saw David as his son. Samuel saw a shepherd boy but God saw a king. It does not matter what man sees. What matters is what God sees. I have a big vision but I have an even bigger God.

I have laid my past aside and have accepted the call, spoken it out, learned what God has brought to me and I am still learning. I will learn until Jesus comes for me. I have gone where He sent me and I fully expect that when I strike the waters they will part because my job is striking them, God's job is parting them. Hallelujah! He always gets the hard part.

Abraham was the father of one yet God made him the father of many nations. David was a shepherd boy yet God made him a king and said he was a man after His own heart. Esther was a young Jewish woman yet God made her a queen so that she could save her people. Peter was an unlearned fisherman but God saw an apostle and when his shadow would pass by people would be healed. Saul was a killer of Christians but God saw Paul the apostle who wrote the majority of the New Testament.

It does not matter what others see or even what you see. What matters is what God sees. Begin to speak faith over yourself and your family. Your victory is wrapped up in your faith. It is impossible to worship God and hate yourself. God says that you were fearfully and wonderfully made. So you messed up, many others did too. Peter denied Christ three times. Paul killed Christians. Let's get this into perspective. If God can forgive Peter and Paul, and He did, then He can forgive you and He can forgive me. I do not deserve anything except death but thankfully God made a way. He sent His son to die for me and for you. Not because we are special but because Jesus was special. Remember we are what God says we are. It does not matter what anyone else says we are. Just don't think too highly of yourself. Where you are going there is no room for false humility. You can be a worm if you want to but praise God I have been set free and my destination is heaven and my trip is orchestrated by God who loves me. What is your destination?

I am a mighty woman of God. I am the head of a world-wide ministry. I am a preacher, teacher, writer, minister of prayer and deliverance. I spread the gospel, cast out demons, heal the sick, and raise the dead [the last hasn't happened yet but it will, because God is God.]

Speaking out faith takes courage and boldness not brashness. I once had plenty of brashness but now I have boldness to say what God says

> § Ask God to change the way you are praying to speak out His will from His perspective.

and accept it as truth. Hallelujah! God is not a man that He should lie and He said to call those things that be not as though they were. Amen. I refuse to accept the lie that the devil has planted outside and inside many churches. The lie of unbelief is more accepted than the truth of God's Word.

I am determined to finish this race and I desire to hear my Lord say, "Well done good and faithful servant." The victory that has overcome the world is our faith!

§
The victory that has overcome the world is our faith!

1. Do you speak faith? Give an example.

2. What area is God telling you needs correction?

3. What steps has He told you to make to align yourself with Him and His Word?

4. Who does God say you are? And what does He have for you to do? (You may not know a lot yet, just write the part that you are sure of, God will broaden it out later. That is His job.)

"Why do you call me Lord, Lord and do not do what I say?"

1 John 5:14-15 *"Now this is the confidence that we have in Him, that if we ask anything according to His will, He hears us. And if we know that He hears us, whatever we ask, we know that we have the petitions that we have asked of Him."*

> § According to His will is according to His Word.

According to His will is according to His Word. God will not tell you to do something or want something that is not in accordance with His Word. This verse explains how you can pray with confidence and expect the answer that you are praying for. The first rule is to pray with confidence and to pray the answer not the problem.

Say you have a daughter that is out in the world. First thank God for her. Then bind the demons and command them to stop manifesting. Then ask God to release the Holy Spirit upon her with the godly opposite of what you just bound up. Then speak out the answer that she would be saved and turned around completely. Thank God for the answer. We have seen this many times with daughters as well as with sons.

Since you are standing in the gap for her, do this at least once every day until you get a release from God in your spirit then as she changes your prayer for her changes. You cannot be lazy and fight the battles. Get up and spend time with God, then attack the enemy and get them off your loved ones.

As you spend time with the Father and in His Word, it is very easy to know His will. He wants you saved, delivered, healed, prosperous, and mature so that you can reproduce in others what God has done for you.

Every day put on your armor! It is good practice, it is necessary, and it is as much a reality as the clothes you put on every day. Here is an example prayer:

I ask You, Father, to search my heart and if there is any uncleanness in me, I ask You to reveal it and I on purpose cast out that work of darkness in the name of Jesus. I put on the Helmet of Salvation and I thank You Father that the same mind that was in Christ is in me. I wrap that Breastplate of Righteousness around me which is based on the shedding of the blood of Jesus and I dedicate my heart to the Lord Jesus and I do not have a divided heart. But I have a heart that praises and worships Him all the days of my life. I place that Belt of Truth around my waist which is the Truth of the Word of God. I thank You, Father that my feet are Shod with the Preparation of the spreading of the Gospel of the Lord Jesus. So I know the Word of God and I am ready

to share with anyone that You bring across my path. I raise up the Shield of Faith that stops all the fiery darts of the enemy as Your Word states. You have given me authority over all the power of the enemy and it will by no means harm me, hallelujah! (Luke 10:19) The Sword of the Spirit is in my other hand which is the powerful Word of God that You have exalted above Your name, in Jesus' name I pray. (Psalm 138:2b)

Thank and praise God for all that He is and all that He does. Bind the enemy from you, your family, your finances, and whatever else God places on you that needs protection. Break all word curses and soulish prayers that are coming against you and command all demons associated with those curses and soulish prayers to leave at once. A soulish prayer is a prayer prayed by a Christian, maybe a well-meaning Christian, that is praying their will not God's will and it loosens demons with it instead of angels. A word curse is someone who is using scripture incorrectly over you or speaking out some form of negativity over you. When I totally surrendered to the Holy Spirit and God began to separate me from people who did not believe the way that I did I am positive that they prayed soulish prayers for me which were really against me. I broke those and cast them down out of the mouths of those who spoke it and commanded all demons to leave me, my family, our property and possessions, and the call on our lives in Jesus' name.

Speak positive scriptures over yourself and your family. Ask God for the vision that He has for your life and the lives of your family. Begin to pray them and see them in your spirit. Use two or three scriptures as a basis for your prayer.

I hope in this book that you have learned who God is, who Jesus is, and who the Holy Spirit is. They are three yet one. Hallelujah! I hope you have also learned who the enemy is and that Jesus defeated him on the cross. That does not mean that we stop fighting. We do not stop fighting until Jesus comes back.

You have learned about the keys to the kingdom and believer's authority. That Jesus has told us to go forth and spread the gospel, cast out demons, heal the sick and raise the dead.

You have learned about worship and how warfare and worship go together. You have learned to listen to the Holy Spirit through His voice, pictures in your mind or through the Word. You have learned that the only way to walk out this life in victory is to first die to self then surrender and obey.

§
We do not stop fighting until Jesus comes back.

> § Prayer is the key to a victorious life.

You have learned how to see the war and how to set the captives free. You learned about a covenant and that God is a covenant keeping God. You have learned about healing and prosperity which are God's promise to us. You have learned how to recognize the enemy and to keep the warring mindset so that you do not fall into his traps. You have learned how to be vigilant in prayer and how to prepare for new territory and new battle strategies. I pray that you have gotten excited about prayer and realized that prayer is the key to a victorious life.

You should also know how to pray with faith and confidence knowing who God is and what His will is. As you put this knowledge to work for you and your family you will see miracles.

Matthew 21:12-15 "*Then Jesus went into the temple of God and drove out all those who bought and sold in the temple, and overturned the tables of the money changers and the seats of those who sold doves. And He said to them, "It is written, 'My house shall be called a house of prayer,' but you have made it a 'den of thieves.'" Then the blind and the lame came to Him in the temple, and He healed them. But when the chief priests and scribes saw the wonderful things that He did, and the children crying out in the temple and saying, "Hosanna to the Son of David!" they were indignant.*"

> § When deliverance comes to the house of God those who believe like a child will rejoice and miracles will happen.

When deliverance comes to the house of God those who believe like a child will rejoice and miracles will happen. Immediately after Jesus delivered the temple (our bodies are temples) the miracles happened. The blind and lame came and they were healed but the religious people got indignant. When deliverance comes to the temple so will signs and wonders. Hallelujah! Jesus is King.

We are going to review all that you have learned. If you need to go back and answer questions, it will refresh your memory.

1. Write out the scripture that has impacted you the most in this study and memorize it.

2. Write an explanation about Who God, Jesus, and the Holy Spirit are as if you were explaining Them to an unsaved person. Use scriptures.

§
Live your life expecting to see miracles.

3. Why does God deserve your worship and praise?

4. Who is the enemy?

5. Who has access to your mind?

6. What did Jesus' death and resurrection do for you?

7. What are the keys of the kingdom? How do you use them?

8. What is believer's authority?

9. Are you better at seeing warfare? Write an example.

10. What is a covenant? What are some of God's covenant promises to us?

11. Has God given you a vision? Put it in a prayer form with scriptures, and write it down.

It has been such a joy to write this book and I hope that it has blessed your life. Please do not allow tradition or religion to keep you from a life of fullness that you can have if you only believe.

Read these scriptures every day for yourself and your family and insert your name and theirs. I did this each day for my husband and sons for at least a year. God's Word works. God is able to do exceedingly abundantly above what I could think or ask according to the power that I am walking in and have allowed to work through me. Get excited, get passionate about Jesus, and see yourself and your world change by the power of the Holy Spirit.

Ephesians 1:17-20 *"that the God of our Lord Jesus Christ, the Father of glory, may give to you the spirit of wisdom and revelation in the knowledge of Him, the eyes of your understanding being enlightened; that you may know what is the hope of His calling, what are the riches of the glory of His inheritance in the saints, and what is the exceeding greatness of His power toward us who believe, according to the*

working of His mighty power which He worked in Christ when He raised Him from the dead and seated Him at His right hand in the heavenly places,"

Ephesians 3:14-20 *"For this reason I bow my knees to the Father of our Lord Jesus Christ, from whom the whole family in heaven and earth is named, that He would grant you, according to the riches of His glory, to be strengthened with might through His Spirit in the inner man, that Christ may dwell in your hearts through faith; that you, being rooted and grounded in love, may be able to comprehend with all the saints what is the width and length and depth and height-- to know the love of Christ which passes knowledge; that you may be filled with all the fullness of God. Now to Him who is able to do exceedingly abundantly above all that we ask or think, according to the power that works in us."*

WORSHIP WITHOUT WARFARE IS NOT UNDERSTANDING AUTHORITY. WARFARE WITHOUT WORSHIP GENERATES TRUSTING IN SELF.

www.ingramcontent.com/pod-product-compliance
Lightning Source LLC
Chambersburg PA
CBHW080446110426
42743CB00016B/3291